Other Jossey-Bass Leadership and Nonprofit Management Titles:

Forging Nonprofit Alliances, *Jane Arsenault*

Creating Your Employee Handbook, *The Management Center, Leyna Bernstein, author*

The Drucker Foundation Self-Assessment Tool for Nonprofit Organizations, Revised Edition, *The Peter F. Drucker Foundation for Nonprofit Management*

Strategic Planning for Public and Nonprofit Organizations, *John M. Bryson*

Marketing Nonprofit Programs and Services, *Douglas B. Herron*

The Jossey-Bass Guide to Strategic Communications for Nonprofits, *Kathleen Bonk, Henry Griggs, Emily Tynes*

The Leader of the Future, *Frances Hesselbein, Marshall Goldsmith, Richard Beckhard, editors*

The Organization of the Future, *Frances Hesselbein, Marshall Goldsmith, Richard Beckhard, editors*

The Community of the Future, *Frances Hesselbein, Marshall Goldsmith, Richard Beckhard, Richard F. Schubert, editors*

Leading Beyond the Walls, *Frances Hesselbein, Marshall Goldsmith, Iain Somerville, editors*

The Collaboration Challenge: How Nonprofits and Businesses Succeed Through Strategic Alliances, *James E. Austin*

Leader to Leader Journal
Leader to Leader: Enduring Insights on Leadership from the Drucker Foundation's Award-Winning Journal, *Frances Hesselbein, Paul Cohen, editors*

Smart Communities

How Citizens and Local Leaders
Can Use Strategic Thinking to
Build a Brighter Future

Suzanne W. Morse

JOSSEY-BASS
A Wiley Imprint
www.josseybass.com

Published by Jossey-Bass
A Wiley Imprint
989 Market Street, San Francisco, CA 94103-1741   www.josseybass.com

Jossey-Bass books and products are available through most bookstores. To contact Jossey-Bass directly call our Customer Care Department within the U.S. at 800-956-7739, outside the U.S. at 317-572-3986, or fax 317-572-4002.

Jossey-Bass also publishes its books in a variety of electronic formats. Some content that appears in print may not be available in electronic books.

Readers should be aware that Internet Web sites listed in this work may have changed or disappeared between when this work was written and when it is read.

The epigraphs by Wilma Mankiller in Chapter 1, John Gardner in Chapter 2, William Winter in Chapter 3, Anne Ganey in Chapter 5, John Jacob in Chapter 7, and Paul Light in Chapter 8 are reprinted with the permission of the University of Richmond in Virginia on behalf of the Pew Partnership for Civic Change.

The epigraph by Becky Anderson in Chapter 4 is reprinted with her permission.

The epigraph in Chapter 6, printed courtesy of the Birmingham Civil Rights Institute, is their organizational tagline.

Library of Congress Cataloging-in-Publication Data

Morse, Suzanne W. (Suzanne Whitlock)
    Smart communities: how citizens and local leaders can use strategic thinking to build a brighter future/ Suzanne W. Morse. —1st ed.
        p. cm.
    Includes bibliographical references and index.
    ISBN 0-7879-6516-2 (alk. paper)
1. Community leadership. 2. Community organization.   I. Title.
    HM781.M67 2004
    307—dc22

                                                                                    2003027951

Printed in the United States of America
FIRST EDITION
HB Printing   10 9 8 7 6 5 4 3 2 1

Contents

Preface

In 1972, Yogi Berra and his wife, Carmen, were on their way to the Baseball Hall of Fame in Cooperstown, New York. As the hours rolled on and the sites stayed unfamiliar, Yogi tried to put Carmen's mind to rest by saying, "We're lost but we're making good time" (1998, p. 51). Although efficiency is a poor substitute for being lost, it provides a good metaphor for thinking about the future of communities. We tend to do three things as we contemplate change: we just keep driving in the same direction and hope we will get there; we refuse to ask directions; or worst of all, we blame our situation on the map, the navigator, or the state highway department. In other words, for too many communities, the future just happens. It is time to think strategically about the roads and the routes that will take communities and citizens where they want to go. History and experience have taught us that some communities do better than others. Abundant educational resources, natural beauty, or a nice climate may help, but they alone do not provide the ticket to success. Could it be that some places are just luckier than others?

The Idea for the Book

This book has been in my mind for much of the last twenty years. After having a front-row seat watching community change, first at the Kettering Foundation and then at the Pew Partnership for Civic

Change, I have seen "lucky" communities of all sizes tackle tough issues and win. I wanted to write a practical book to help communities improve their chances of success while using the resources at their disposal.

Travels to hundreds of cities have given me the rare privilege of seeing communities up close. My observations over the years have guided the development of the *smart-decisions framework*. To be sure, I have never visited a perfect community. All places have challenges. However, success is much more likely to follow from actions and practices originating within communities than from almost any external force. To say unequivocally that communities control their own destiny is too strong. It would be naïve and presumptuous to believe that we do not need strong, proactive public policies that support communities and the people who live in them. Having said that, I can also say that some communities are able to manage their challenges more effectively than others. It is not serendipity or blind luck. These communities have a sense of where the community wants to go and some strong ideas on how it will get there. Dependence on outside people or outside resources is not a long-term strategy for sustainability.

More than a decade of research by the Pew Partnership for Civic Change, focusing on the elements of community success, has yielded some very specific steps required for successful change. The foundation of this book is built on the collective wisdom of hundreds of communities and thousands of civic leaders who have implemented the steps to success profiled in *Smart Communities*. As too many have wistfully waited for the silver bullet of an economic development strategy or an elected leader, these "lucky" communities have tackled tough issues and won. So how have they done it? The answer in every case was their ability to see the big picture and to make strategic decisions. In his book *The Fifth Discipline*, Peter Senge says that "tackling a difficult problem is often a matter of seeing where the high leverage lies, a change which—with minimum effort—would lead to lasting, significant improvement" (1990, p. 65).

In 1992, the Pew Partnership for Civic Change began its search for community leverage points through partnerships with fourteen smaller cities, ranging in population from 50,000 to 150,000. We believed that smaller cities could be "laboratories" for learning more about civic success. For example, Santa Fe, New Mexico, was faced with a serious affordable-housing shortage. Citizens in Waco, Texas, knew that they must find safe, productive places for young people to go after school. And residents of Danville, Virginia, needed to think about their economic future with the decline in textiles and tobacco in the region. In each of these communities, and in the eleven others that were part of the initiative, there has been significant, transferable learning on ways to improve the results on major social issues.

As I began to look at the key strategies used by our most successful partners, seven *high-leverage points* began to emerge as critical to community change. Although the issues were different, the ways of working were not. Communities that were having success were doing the following:

- Investing right the first time

- Working together

- Building on community strengths

- Practicing democracy

- Preserving the past

- Growing leaders

- Inventing a brighter future

Sounds like a simple list. In reality, however, it is hard for communities to change how they operate, whom they include, and who makes the decisions. Communities need an everyday strategy that produces better decisions and also builds a stronger sense of community for all who live there. These seven leverage points provide the framework for change. *Smart Communities* is ultimately about strategic thinking and acting. Although it is cast in the context of real issues and real places, its main purpose is to highlight new ways that communities can organize their collective work for the long term.

So what is a smart community? It is a geographical place, a set of interests, or a group of people that has invented a process of work that includes, discusses, anticipates, and acts on its critical common issues, building on its assets, its broad-based leadership, and its history and values.

A Strategy for Success

The civic landscape is filled with well-meaning approaches to change. Community leaders have worked tirelessly to change the outcomes for their communities. However, despite the mounds of research on the chronic nature of most problems, the huge investments of resources on our most intractable problems, and the legions of really smart people taking a turn at solving them, we don't see a level of change that satisfies anybody. Poverty rates are still too high, too many children and young adults are left behind *forever*, and external forces like drugs, gangs, and street crime continue to dominate too many communities. So what needs to happen for communities to operate differently?

The short answer is that we must make better decisions. Places that invest early and for the long term, that include diverse viewpoints and multiple stakeholders in the problem-solving process, that create a vision of what could be, and finally that take collective action *always* get better results. This book identifies the strategic elements that every community needs to make decisions that create a better future for everyone.

Smart Communities differs from other community building books in key ways. First, it embeds process into results. In a sense, the book works backwards. The profiles provide an application of a particular leverage point from a results perspective, not just from process. Second, the book moves out of big cities to examine the work of smaller cities and rural areas. If we are really to learn how to change communities, we must cast a wider net for ideas and decisions that make a difference. Third, this book is written with an unshakable belief that residents want to improve their communities and *can*. For years, I have been squarely in the camp of those Americans who believe that citizens are still engaged in where they live. Every community has a plethora of people who have not given up, who work tirelessly, and who still believe in their community. If we can put a human being on the moon and a cell phone in nearly every hand, I am convinced that we can make significant inroads on poverty and race relations, and give a good start to every child.

Finally, *Smart Communities* is organized for action. Each of the seven leverage points is introduced with a brief summary of the research in the field that frames the discussion, then followed by illustrations of successful applications of the leverage points. Each chapter concludes with practical next steps for you to take. The profiles used in *Smart Communities* are not about locked-tight successes or full-fledged case studies. They provide a specific lens on a way of thinking and making decisions to help you think differently about decisions in your own community. In some examples, the result is clear—a downtown restored or a civic process created—but in most others, the smart decisions fall on a continuum of change. The illustrations used are less about "good" programs than about the insights that influenced the decision-making process. There are no gold standard formulas, as you will read, but there are tested paths to change that have been and are being traveled. There are directions to follow that can get better results.

The biggest challenge in writing the book was not the identification of the "smart" decisions; several volumes could be filled up with those. The problem was finding the right chapter for the case illustrations. Almost all the community decisions described in the book could have been discussed with the perspective of a different chapter and a different point of view. In other words, these communities and hundreds more are doing many things right and in many venues. Ultimately, the search was for well-structured decision-making processes that built on the seven key leverage points. It was a challenge for the research team to discuss only one angle of their civic life. Further, we were not looking for the nitty-gritty missteps (in most cases). What you will read about are actions taken that resulted in successful outcomes.

Who Should Read the Book

Smart Communities is for all those who have a say—or want a say—in the decisions affecting their community. These people go by names such as citizen, teacher, mayor, city councilor, business leader, nonprofit executive, religious leader, student, editor, superintendent, hospital administrator, parent, and a whole host of others in the community who want to find new ways of thinking about old problems. This book shows a new strategy for organizing our collective work for better results.

The ideas will be most effective if the concepts are read and understood by more than a few people in the community. They can prompt a conversation about how these leverage points have been used previously in the community and to what end. They should raise questions about what needs to change. This is not a solo conversation. To be smart, communities have to act smart. That requires joint action and new thinking.

The book can be particularly helpful to new board members and newly elected or appointed public officials. The illustrations included will help them invent the right wheel (not reinvent) for their particular community, tailoring it to specific circumstances. The illustrations are prods for thinking about how to create a different path.

Likewise, students from a variety of disciplines—urban studies, sociology, education, and political science—will see in real time how inclusive planning, timely investments, and asset identification can collectively create a scenario for change that forever alters the future of a community. Public-administration students can better understand the role that public administrators and elected leaders can play as catalysts for change, not just the voice of the status quo.

Finally, the book provides strategies for "moving over" to existing leaders from every sector. It is time to allow more people to sit at the community table. This can only happen in environments that encourage new voices to be heard. A wonderful anecdote told by Industrial Areas Foundation organizer Gerald Taylor illustrates the need to think in practical ways and hear new voices. The "Accident Ministry" was a major outreach program of a rural congregation. The church was located on a winding rural road, with little signage for approaching cars. Inevitably, as traffic would increase near the beginning of services, the expected loud crash would follow. The congregation saw this as a ministerial opportunity and had uniformed congregation members run to the scene with limited medical supplies and the religious message of the morning. They were "ministering and administering" at the same time. As the years wore on, however, there was a dilemma: the congregation had grown so much that there were more accidents before each service; the original Accident Ministry team was getting too old to run as fast as was needed; and there was a lack of interest by younger people to take the job. The alternatives for the future success of the Accident Ministry were being discussed and debated after services one Sunday when a young voice from the back of the room asked a defining question, "Why don't we just straighten the road?"

This book is ultimately for those citizens, local government officials, business leaders, and nonprofit executives who want to straighten the road in their communities. The individuals and organizations profiled in the book addressed the problem, whatever it was, and took action. They did not gloss over its negative impact, wring their hands, or blame the navigators. They took responsibility and made smart decisions. They did what needed to be done to solve the problem or seize an opportunity. They listened. *Smart Communities* is aimed at people who want directions to their destination: those that are unwilling to keep going down the same road.

Identifying the Case Studies

In addition to developing the seven leverage points, we had to think about the kinds of community profiles that best illustrate them. The communities discussed are tackling some of the toughest problems in society—school dropouts, broken neighborhoods, a sinking economy—and they will continue to tackle these issues over time. Others are creating new vehicles for partnership, public deliberation, and asset-based development. Why these topics and not others? The issues are illustrations of the broad range of things that a community must consider as it invents new ways of working together. There are many other weighty issues. The cases are snapshots, not the whole picture of any community. There is only one exception to this generalized approach to the issues profiled: dropouts. When we were beginning the book, the research team, perhaps like many of you, had not given much thought to the high school dropout issue. I certainly hadn't. But as we delved more into the issues facing cities and their prospects for success, it became clear to us that this was an issue on which many others turned. You will read more background on this issue than on the others. It is a complicated issue but not an unbeatable one. The first step for any community member to take is to find out the extent of the problem and then probe its impact on other issues, such as jobs, social services, and crime. This issue got our attention, and I suspect it will get yours as well.

We used a variety of scans in selecting communities. First, we looked at the national indicators—ranging from the "top-rated" lists of national magazines, to the Annie E. Casey Kids Count profiles, to U.S. census data. Some communities kept coming up on all types of indices. For example, Iowa got high marks from all the indicators, so we began to look more deeply to find out why. We also interviewed people in a range of disciplines and professions to get ideas. Finally, we just looked at the facts. Some cities are just doing better than others. But we had another criterion: we were looking for the unsung heroes. Some cities are just "hot" these days. We respect them and the work being done there, but we wanted to dig a little deeper into the American landscape. We also wanted to include rural America and identify the struggles and successes being made in small places with big issues. We were not on the search for perfection as in the "best" cities for anything. The people making the key decisions in the places profiled in this book will tell you that their structure was not perfect. They were trying to think smart and act strategically on some of the toughest issues facing our society, without a roadmap in some cases. However, these ideas and actions and the creativity they generated have come from people from every part of the community in every region of the country. Finally, we fully acknowledge that the illustrations are just that. The stories are told to exemplify a particularly successful strategy. In all instances, the case is much more complex and the road to success circuitous and complicated.

Overview of the Contents

Each chapter in the book includes an introduction to and a definition of the particular leverage point, a collection of case studies that illustrate the leverage point in action, and a final "getting started" section that points the reader to some basic next steps.

Chapter One, Setting the Stage for Community Change, provides the background for the seven leverage points. We take a quick tour of American communities to determine how they have developed and what they might learn from one another. With the advent of television and the World Wide Web, many places that were isolated from mainstream America have felt both pleasure and pain from their new proximity to one another. No community is immune to the negative or positive influences of the connected world. As the news media take us from one coast to another on a nightly basis, we sort of forget about the space in between, which includes places from Almena to Zanesville.

Chapter Two, Investing Right the First Time, examines strategies for community investing. There are many issues that are potential community investments. Communities have to weigh priorities and the anticipated return on certain investments. Specifically, we look at a particular community issue, dropout prevention, an issue that has far-reaching effects on a whole community. We suggest ways that communities can begin and maintain a thoughtful process to ensure that they are making timely decisions on the issues that matter most.

Chapter Three, Working Together, profiles the kinds of decisions that galvanize and redefine community processes. In a world of fences and barriers, the smartest communities are finding ways to work together across fault lines and county lines. Reaching the collective potential of a community requires the inclusion of a multitude of ideas and voices. These processes have different names, such as partnership and collaboration, but the outcome is the same: realization that our futures are intertwined.

Chapter Four, Building on Community Strengths, puts community decision making in the context of asset-based development. In particular, we examine how several communities have been able to identify and build on their individual, organizational, institutional, and physical assets and get very positive results. Emphasizing assets over deficits can change a community's odds for the future as well as change the lens for those outside the community.

Chapter Five, Practicing Democracy, examines the ideas, circumstances, and processes that bring citizens back into democracy. No longer can we count on experts to "fix" things for us; a major responsibility rests with citizens to help guide the way for community change. Dialogue, public deliberation, and inclusion are not luxuries in a democracy but rather are necessary components of action. For change to happen, people must be able to organize themselves to act. Dialogue and deliberation are the processes that make action happen.

Chapter Six, Preserving the Past, illustrates ways that communities are preserving their past with buildings, history, and culture and how those are informing the future. Preservation can build communities physically, economically, and civically. Communities can learn how to position themselves for future success by not forgetting their past.

Chapter Seven, Growing Leaders, looks at the broad-based leadership that is necessary in communities if positive change is to occur. Old patterns of civic involvement and governance won't work. We need strong leadership from every sector, and our continuing challenge is for leadership that is broad, deep, and ready to work together. Communities have multitudes of people prepared and willing to contribute more. They need to find them and put them to work.

Chapter Eight, Inventing a Brighter Future, synthesizes the previous leverage points as vehicles for inventing the future. Just as inventors and innovative mechanics use bailing wire and glue to make things go, so do citizens. There are sophisticated models that have been evaluated and assessed for reliability and validity, but there are also some "necessity" inventions that are doing the job. There is a need to know about both and about how to become "inventing communities."

Communities that incorporate the seven leverage points profiled in this book greatly improve their chances of "being smart" over the long run. Too many communities are stymied by the past or intimidated by the future. They need not be. Even if things have gone wrong or mistakes have been made, this is an opportunity for reflection, new ways of working, and most of all, action. But like Yogi Berra, they need a map.

Smart Communities provides directions for strategic decision making. Communities will always be faced with issues related to external policies and funding, prior decisions that have to be addressed, and ongoing and unexpected challenges. There will always be both problems and opportunities. This book is a guide to manage both in smarter ways. As sociologist David Riesman once said, America is the land of second chances (Potter, 1996, p. viii). This book is a blueprint for second chances to make smart decisions.

Charlottesville, Virginia   Suzanne W. Morse
January 2004

Acknowledgments

A number of years ago, I asked a gifted writer how he knew so much about the topics of his books. He replied that he didn't know much about the subjects at first; that is why he wrote the books. I knew in beginning this book that I had much to learn and I was right. I had some strong hunches about how successful communities came to be after almost three decades of asking the question, but it was the people I met while writing the book that added certainty to those hunches.

I want to thank the many people who willingly gave their time and ideas during interviews over the last year. Some names appear in the book, but there are many others not listed whose reflections on community were invaluable. Not a single person declined my request for an interview. Each of you taught me about community decision making, but more important, you inspired me with your example.

My appreciation goes particularly to my colleagues at The Pew Charitable Trusts who have encouraged and supported the writing of this book: Rebecca Rimel, president; Don Kimelman, director of the Venture Fund; and Suzanne Biemiller, then program officer in the Venture Fund. Also my thanks to the staff of the Pew Partnership for Civic Change—Jacqueline Dugery, Jim Knowles, Sharon Siler, and Carole Hamner Schmidt—for assuming more responsibilities and allowing me the time and space to complete the book.

This book could not have been completed without an enormously gifted research team that helped at every stage: Kathleen Grammatico Ferraiolo, Claiborne Walthall, Michael Briand, Monica Gillespie, and Jim Knowles. They researched, they wrote, they critiqued, and they deliberated on the style and content of the book. Some of the best ideas in the book are theirs; the mistakes are all mine. Several of the team members took the lead on specific case studies: Kathleen Grammatico Ferraiolo (Cedar Rapids, Dallas, and Charlottesville), Claiborne Walthall (Lowell), and Michael Briand (Jacksonville, Owensboro, and Hampton). Thanks also to Peggy Powell and Nora Gibson for typing the manuscripts and for cheerfully and accurately interpreting many handwritten pages.

Thanks especially to my editor at Jossey-Bass, Johanna Vondeling. She has been an invaluable source of encouragement and advice at every step of the writing process. Her even hand and attention to task made this book a reality. Appreciation goes also to Allison Brunner for her editorial expertise and to Ocean Howell, who gave the book proposal early support and focus.

Smart Communities has been influenced by many smart people. My parents, Glenn and Etta Whitlock, and sister, Doris Hixon, have been stellar examples of what civic engagement really means. Norman Cousins, John Gardner, and David Mathews have been more than mentors. They taught me about the possibilities of community.

Finally, to my husband, Ned Moomaw; our son, Will Moomaw; and our daughters, Betsy Peyton and Amy Goodnight, a special word of thanks for all your patience and support during the time spent working and not playing.

—S.W.M.

The Author

Suzanne W. Morse is the executive director of the Pew Partnership for Civic Change, a civic research organization that identifies and disseminates solutions to the nation's toughest challenges. She is also a fellow at the Jepson School of Leadership Studies, University of Richmond. Before founding the Pew Partnership in 1993, she spent the previous nine years at the Kettering Foundation.

Morse has spent her career addressing issues critical to strong democratic communities. She has written extensively on the subject of civic leadership, and her research has appeared in numerous national publications. She serves as a trustee of the Kettering Foundation and the Topsfield Foundation and on the national advisory boards of the LBJ School of Public Affairs at the University of Texas, and the Hart Leadership Program, Duke University. She was awarded the Content of Our Character Generational Ethics Award in 2002. She received her doctorate from the University of Alabama. Morse lives with her husband and son in Charlottesville, Virginia.

1

Setting the Stage for Community Change

> *I think a healthy community is one where people are*
> *not just out for themselves, and they are not just*
> *working on their individual pursuits, but where they*
> *understand their relationship and responsibility to*
> *other people.*
>
> *Wilma Mankiller*

As communities and citizens look to one another for answers to the most compelling social questions of our time, they need a wide-angle lens. American communities are broad and deep. They range from Almena, Wisconsin (population 720), to Tupelo, Mississippi (population 35,000), to Portland, Oregon, (population 529,000) (U.S. Bureau of the Census, 2000). Citizens in each of those communities, and hundreds like them, have ideas—good ideas—that need to be understood, tailored, communicated, and acted upon. However, among this variegated landscape of what we call community, there are no perfect ones. Even those with flowing fountains, rehabilitated Main Streets, and robust economies still have issues to address.

Framing the Issues

This chapter sets the stage for the seven leverage points. It gives a glimpse of urban development and its modern-day implications. We know that the community building progress is never linear. Some of the early American cities that started strong have faltered; new places have sprung up seemingly overnight. The important variable is how communities managed their inevitable change.

Success does not happen by chance. It can occur for different reasons. Sometimes it is the "right place at the right time" phenomenon, but most often it is a combination of forces. Good decisions at critical times carry the day for the future. They can be headline catchers, but more likely they are day-to-day actions of people in the community that reflect a value system and a way of working.

Communities Come in All Sizes

The term *community* is used throughout this book to limit the use of stratifying terms, like *urban, rural, suburban, region,* or just *city.* Those are real and tangible classifications, but rarely does one hear, "I am working to make my suburb better." People live in communities. They may be high-rise, low-rise, dangerous, safe, attractive, littered—but people still live there.

Community is a term that is used very specifically on the one hand and very casually on the other. Community evolves around three nexuses: the community of relationships, the community of interests, and the community of place. When the famed Frenchman Alexis de Tocqueville visited America in the nineteenth century, he was impressed by the associational life of Americans: by their connections to activities and organizations—*their relationships,* by the common concerns that bound them together—*their interests,* but also by the propensity to talk over the back fence on issues of

mutual concern—*their place*. The connections and interrelation-
ships of community allowed for a stronger and more vibrant civic
life. This view of nineteenth-century life may be a simplistic over-
statement of civic life as we know it. It is easier to think in "common" terms when our geographical space is well-defined and our
relational interests clear. It is not so easy when cultures clash and
interests conflict. In nineteenth-century America, it was likely that
a person knew the neighbor on the other side of the fence. Today
it is important to both understand and build on our varying definitions and new expressions of community.

Modern-day community life is hard to isolate and to generate.
Boundaries, from city limit signs to fire districts to backyard fences,
don't tell the whole story. Our lives and fortunes are entangled in
ways that de Tocqueville could never have imagined. Suburbs are
no longer just that—they are inner ring and outer ring, and they
respond to the central city and one another in unique ways. Rural
areas abut major metropolitan areas and are accessible to them by
a short car or train ride. Small cities connect to other small cities
to create regional presence.

Identifying common interests within and between communities
of place, however, is the name of the game. We cannot separate ourselves from one another no matter how hard we try. The suburbs
have a stake in the central city; cities have a stake in the suburbs;
and rural areas are affected by cities and regions. Places that can
establish strong identities for themselves while developing relationships with their neighbors hold the greatest promise for economic, social, and civic success.

Now what are communities? They are where individuals live,
connect, and are responsible for one another. Sometimes they
are called cities, like Denver; sometimes they are called regions,
like western North Carolina; sometimes they are called cultures, like
Hmong; and sometimes they are just called home, like Almena,
Wisconsin.

What We Know About Communities

The more than 280 million people who live in America live in communities of all sizes (U.S. Bureau of the Census, 2000). Jacksonville, Florida, has a land mass of 841 square miles and a population of 736,000. New York City has a land mass of 304 square miles and a population of over 8 million. Table 1.1 shows the diversity of size that challenges any definition of community. Within this broad spectrum, we know that all places share promise and peril. Extraordinarily poor people live in all kinds of communities—rural farms and high-rise apartments. Economic downturns hit cities, suburbs, and small towns without favor.

Although the nation's urban policy has never directed America's population to be spread between places of all sizes, that is exactly what has happened. As a nation, by our patterns of settlement, we have taken the stand that we do not want to be a country of just major hubs with fast-food restaurants in between. Even in the early establishment of the nation, citizens found themselves moving toward less populated areas for both space and opportunities. The slogan "Go west, young man" represented not only a desire to move out of the populated northeast but also the need for more opportunity. Consciously or not, we have put a premium on the diversity of communities and what they offer.

There has always been a proverbial clash between American values and "way of life" as it relates to cities. Historically, many Americans were afraid of the negative aspects of cities. Even today, opinion polls show that Americans say that they would prefer to live in a small town. Yet when asked additional questions about what they value in their quality-of-life index, they respond with such things as access to medical care, culture, and business opportunities (Abbott, 1992, p. 115). This ambivalence has been both the boom and the bust of cities. People are quite attracted to the glitter and access of cities but prefer to locate themselves and their families far enough away to avoid the negative aspects of cities, and

Table 1.1.   Where America Lives

Population	Number of Places	Total Population
Under 1,000	11,024	4,446,489
1,000–2,499	5,063	8,256,846
2,500–9,999	5,507	28,138,325
10,000–24,999	2,054	32,174,525
25,000–49,999	838	29,005,785
50,000–249,999	597	54,884,108
250,000–499,999	38	13,702,659
500,000–999,999	20	12,905,864
1,000,000 and above	9	22,947,966

Source: U.S. Bureau of the Census, 2000.

especially higher taxes (p. 119). They want to feel safe, know their neighbors, and have an easy commute but also have the advantages of big-city amenities.

Smaller cities and towns are no longer isolated from the mainstream economic world, which is often associated with big urban areas. They have capitalized on the technology revolution and thrust themselves into the forefront of international business. Distance from the national business epicenters, once considered the death knell of business enterprise, is virtually erased by such now commonplace aids as computers, fax machines, and the Internet.

The last two decades have also seen a sharpening of our understanding of community "writ large," so to speak. We now think in local as well as regional contexts. Historically, we have thought of cities and their issues by size—cities over a million, cities over 250,000, and so forth. Now we know better. As borders touch and issues run past the city limits signs, we must recalibrate our conception of a city or community and its impact. For the purposes of this book, we will include four general types of communities: urban areas, "metropolitowns," smaller cities and towns, and rural areas. This appears at first glance to be a narrow swath through a large field. There will be little attention to suburbs or to regions—although both are critically important to the health of all sizes of communities. The emphasis is on the core places that people call home or, better said, their home base. The four categories need a little explanation:

- *Urban areas* run the gamut from New York City and Los Angeles on the one end to Atlanta and St. Louis on the other. The division of urban core from suburban ring notwithstanding, this category includes those central cities that have the largest populations, with New York City at the top and Riverside, California, at the end of the list with 255,166 (U.S. Bureau of the Census, 2000).

- *Metropolitowns* are a new category, designated by Pew Partnership research as places with populations of 50,000 to 250,000. They offer the culture, amenities, and resources of large metropolitan areas while preserving a quality of life often associated with small-town living.

- *Small cities and towns* have populations between 10,000 and 49,000. These are often county seats, homes to universities, state capitals, or just places where people live, work, and want their children to stay.

- *Rural areas* are communities under 10,000 and can range down to populations of one single person, according to the 2000 U.S. census.

Size, we have learned, is no guarantee of more interaction among people on issues of common concern; some of the most divided communities are smaller ones. Although we certainly cannot overgeneralize all community problems, I would argue that places of all sizes provide the opportunity to examine issues and remedies with fresh perspectives. Cities, towns, and rural areas have unique circumstances because of size, but there is less validation today for separating the analysis of their issues than four decades ago. Smaller cities, metropolitowns, and even rural areas have new issues to address because of changing demographics, access to transportation, and technology. Communities of all sizes are no longer isolated from centers of commerce. They are aggressive economic developers, competing for the attention of national and international firms, developing sophisticated high-technology parks, repositioning their economies, revitalizing their central business districts, and finding ways to make their communities better.

Place still matters. Despite the whirl of bits and bytes, and the eye-blinking speed of the Internet, people and businesses want to live and work in real communities. Writing in the *Harvard Business Review* (1995), Michael Porter makes a compelling case for having one eye focused on the world and one eye focused at home. In theory, he argues, global markets, advanced technology, and high-speed transportation *should* reduce the role that location plays in business competition. But the opposite is true: a sustainable and competitive economic advantage is rooted in tapping the unique benefits of location. Improving our communities is a critical factor in creating a competitive advantage domestically and globally (p. 58).

A community can be successful attracting new economic development, but it must also have a conducive culture to attract people. In *The Rise of the Creative Class* (2002), Richard Florida writes that creative communities can be the critical variable in attracting the creative class and creative companies to particular areas. There are 38 million Americans who work in science and engineering, architecture, the arts, education, and music and who are looking for places that have a "creative climate," one that values ethnic and cultural diversity, a concentration of younger people, an arts-and-music scene, outdoor recreation, technology, and what is called *third places* (p. 8, pp. 215–234). These third places are neither work nor home, but rather the places that citizens go for less-formal interactions— places such as coffee shops, bookstores, and cafés (Oldenburg, 1989).

In other words, it is not enough to eliminate the negatives; we must also cultivate and invest in the value-added positives. Successful community efforts have found the right combination of community investments and amenities that foster, cultivate, and encourage a different kind of place for community and economic activity. Places such as Austin, San Diego, and Asheville understand this, but so do places like Wilmington, North Carolina, which boasts the largest film production facility east of California. As people in communities look for answers, the ideas and solutions may come from places unlike their own. As the following chapters illustrate, success is neither place- nor size-bound. It comes from a set of seven tested leverage points that help all communities decide their futures.

How Communities Came to Be

Every day's news bombards us with a litany of problems and crises. The good news is that we are not alone; the bad news is that we have dealt with civic concerns since our founding and the problems never seem to go away. Concern over social challenges has been a part of the American psyche from the country's birth. Before and after the American Revolution, colonial cities were growing and becoming more diverse in every respect. Early American communities were ordered both physically and socially, and land was appropriated according to social position and hierarchy. Unfortunately, those early patterns of urban development are alive and thriving today and must still be reckoned with.

Morton and Lucia White (1962) write that after the Civil War, there were increased concerns about the impersonality of the city, the lack of genuine communication, the increased number of immigrants, and "too little continuity of face-to-face relations for the sound and full development of character" (p. 218). The end of the war brought to northern and southern cities alike a major building and rebuilding phase and aided the shift from rural to urban that added to their concerns.

Communities grew in three major stages. The first was gradual, stretching from the colonial era to the early nineteenth century. Cities like Philadelphia (1682), Charleston (1672), and Providence (1636) came into existence in the colonial period. The second stage filled a century from 1820 to 1920 and reflected the industrial boom and westward expansion. This period of rapid urbanization firmly established cities as an integral component of American life. Finally, the third stage, considered the modern urban age, began in the 1920s and continues today. In addition to growth in existing urban areas, this period has seen the creation of cities and the tremendous growth of suburbs surrounding metropolitan areas. In fact, in 1910 the U.S. Census Bureau created the classification *metropolitan district* to use as a vehicle for collecting data on the inhabitants living outside the central city. By 1920, the census found that more than half of the nation's population was urban (Abbott, 1992, p. 111). Today its urban population exceeds 80 percent of the total.

One of the more interesting phenomena of nineteenth- and early twentieth-century America was the *planned community,* or the community of interests and relationships, and settlement patterns it set for the future. There were several types of planned communities: company towns that were developed and built for employees and their families, communities that were built outside the city as an escape from the wear and tear of central-city life, and communities that were built as self-contained entities.

In the first instance, company towns were not new. As the Industrial Revolution took hold in America in the nineteenth century, rows of similar, if not exact, "company" houses were built outside factories, lumberyards, and textile mills. Volumes have been written about life in mill villages. What is unique about some of these planned communities is that the word *community* (though limited) was taken seriously: communities were viewed as something other than housing stock. Two examples of these planned communities are Lowell, Massachusetts, and Pullman, Illinois. In the case of Lowell, a thriving textile town founded in 1822, enlightened self-interest prodded the town and the business owners to provide amenities to the labor force, such as suitable housing for single women as well as for the larger workforce. Lowell typified what could happen in a mill town. Its fortunes turned after 1860, as a later chapter explains, and Lowell began on a downward spiral. However, its modern-day renaissance, one could argue, had its origins in the fact that companies had the capital and political influence to build housing, public buildings, and public parks that later became the rallying cry for preservation. Pullman, Illinois, was the model community of George Pullman of sleeping-car fame. Pullman forbade alcohol (to maintain sobriety), established a library (to encourage serious thought), and maintained all housing as rental units (to control his workforce). At the end of the nineteenth century, labor unrest and economic downturn caused its demise (Abbott, 1992, p. 118). The infrastructure that Pullman had financed later became the pride of the community.

The second type of planned community is the luxurious one often found outside large urban areas. Residential areas like Llewellyn Park, New Jersey; Shaker Heights, Ohio; and Riverside, Illinois, were havens of pastoral security for those who wanted to have the benefits of city life without the hassles. These types of suburban communities illustrated the exodus (although slight at first) of higher-income families out of the central city (Abbott, 1992, p. 118).

Finally, and perhaps the most interesting of the three, are communities of interests and relationships that grew around three ideas: *conviction, culture,* and *discrimination.* The followers of Joseph Smith wanted to practice their religion, Mormonism, with religious freedom in Utah; the Shakers wanted a communal life at Sabbathday Lake and elsewhere. Newly immigrated Chinese bore the brunt of housing discrimination and threat to personal safety and clustered in "Chinatowns" from coast to coast. The African American relocation to northern cities like New York and Chicago was met with many of the same barriers and dangers that occurred in the segregated South. Housing and social-participation options were closed, so they established communities of their own. Harlem was a summer retreat for wealthy white New Yorkers until the late nine-teenth century, when it became one of the few places African Americans could find housing in New York City. "Little Havana" in Miami became a comfortable assimilation place for newly arrived Cuban refugees.

What is important about these particular models of planned communities is their transference to modern circumstances. What can be inferred, for then as well as now, is that urban isolationism is difficult if not impossible to sustain. Short of a walled city, every American community is open to the influences of a larger area. Sec-ond, suburbs, then and now, take taxpaying, home-owning citizens away from the central city that needs them desperately. Despite their removed location, however, suburbs of all kinds are affected by the changes of fortune in the neighboring central city. As David Rusk (1993) writes in *Cities Without Suburbs*, the relative wealth of suburbs is related to the financial strength of the neighboring cen-tral city. Finally, commercial enterprises located in a city have con-siderable effect on how that community develops and the kinds of amenities and assets it offers. A diversified commerce brings sus-tained vitality to communities of all sizes. Whereas communities dominated by one industry or business benefited when times were good, they have suffered unmercifully in the downturns. Flint, Michigan, a General Motors town through and through, is a living example of the booms and the busts around one industry.

The Growth and Decline of Communities

Historically, as now, both the growth and the decline of communi-ties have been caused by a broad spectrum of factors and circum-stances. In the nineteenth century, westward movement brought population growth west of the Mississippi for a number of reasons. Mining and large parcels of inexpensive farm and ranch land drew people out of the crowded Northeast. A city like Denver, though land- and mountain-locked, grew very rapidly because it was the urban hub for the vast hinterland of ranchers and farmers. The city grew from its beginnings in the mid-nineteenth century to over a hundred thousand by 1890 (Monkkonen, 1988, p. 84).

Jefferson, Texas, in contrast, was the "Riverport to the Southwest" in the mid-nineteenth century, a bustling port where Mississippi River cargo boats loaded and unloaded. In a time before railroads came to north Texas, Jefferson provided the only alternative for importing and exporting for the region. In its heyday, Jefferson was second to Galveston in cargo tonnage shipped from Texas. Jefferson's decline was prompted in part by a decision by the U.S. Corps of Engineers in 1873 to remove a natural barrier on the Red River called the Great Raft, which dropped the water level in the port so that shipping was questionable and no longer profitable. The coming of the railroads completed the demise. Today Jefferson is a quaint town that has built a premier tourist industry around the river and its prestigious past (Jefferson, Texas, Web site).

Some cities remade themselves to appeal to the changing national environment. Southern cities, devastated by the Civil War, began to build back and acquire economic clout. Atlanta was in prime position when the notion of the "Sunbelt" first began to get notice in the 1970s. It became a "world-class city," at its own naming, and began to act like one. As one Georgia trade official commented, "The Sunbelt is not sunshine. It's an attitude . . . conducive to business. The North has lost that attitude." All this boosterism notwithstanding, there has been a resurgence of fortunes of cities from the deep South to the Southwest to the far West (even Oklahoma added a rising-sun logo to the license plates) (Larsen, 1990, pp. 148–150).

Boosterism, however, sometimes works. Duluth, Minnesota, a community at the tip of northern Minnesota, was promoted by its boosters in the nineteenth century as a transportation hub, connecting St. Paul, Chicago, New York, Paris, London, and Calcutta! Certainly a possibility, but not a direct route by any means (Monkkonen, 1988, pp. 83–84). Duluth today is a city of over 85,000 people that counts international shipping among its major industries. It is the largest port on the Great Lakes and one of the premier bulk cargo ports in North America, with more than a thousand ships from many foreign countries docking at the Duluth-Superior port every year. Communities can create image, substance, and their future (Duluth, Minnesota, Web site).

The point, of course, is that the evolution of American communities has been caused by both internal and external factors. The main objective has been to manage those conditions in the most productive way. The places that have done that are still around, perhaps with a different look, because they have taken charge of their future. Others that did not adapt or at least keep up have paid the price economically. None of this is to suggest that communities should follow the latest fad. Neither can they let the future just happen to them. They have to organize themselves for success.

Even though Americans are by nature independent and individualistic, it has become increasingly clear that smart communities must think about the rest of their county or the rest of their region as they craft decisions. The issues and the opportunities facing communities cannot be addressed unilaterally. Solving the crime problem in the inner city or the lack of living-wage jobs needs a region's best thinking and action. Likewise, mounting a major regional economic development effort requires that more than one community or location be involved.

Political reformer Fredrick Howe's notion was that cities were the hope of democracy because of their ability to give a fair start to all people through schools, health, and social services. Despite this hopefulness, challenges presented by cities and towns of all sizes are not new and are not going away. Jane Jacobs wrote in 1961 that there is a wistful myth among us that if we only had enough money, we could wipe out slums in a decade, revitalize aging and seemingly passé neighborhoods, anchor the wandering middle class, and corral the traffic problems. Jacobs sarcastically observes that even with a few billion we seem to have made the problems worse. In her words, "We have not rebuilt cities, we have sacked them" (p. 4). Jacobs is certainly right that money alone will not "fix" problems, but smart investment plus new ways of thinking and working can.

The Mailboxes on Main Street

A growing phenomenon in all communities is their increased diversity. No longer do the mailboxes on Main Street just have names like Smith, Jones, and Washington. They are now interspersed with Gonzales and Rhon. Coastal cities as well as traditionally homogeneous landlocked communities have had a change in their demographic composition.

Shifting demographics are perhaps the most significant change affecting communities in all locales and of all sizes. The melting pot has moved to middle America. Ethnic grocery stores, places of worship, and non-English radio and television abound in previously homogeneous communities. You do not have to go to Little Havana in Miami to attend church services in Spanish. You can go to Allentown, Pennsylvania. Or if you want to understand more about southeast Asian culture, you can visit Wausau, Wisconsin.

According to the 1980 U.S. census, Wausau, Wisconsin, was the most ethnically homogeneous city in the nation, with less than 1 percent of the population nonwhite (Beck, 1994). Wausau has, over the last decade or so, become home to thousands of Hmong immigrants from the mountain tribes of Laos. Hmong children make up a quarter of Wausau's elementary school enrollment, and Asians make up 4.5 percent of the total population of 38,426. A resettlement area for the Lutheran Church, Wausau became home to hundreds of Hmong families fleeing the oppressive government in Laos. In addition to the Laotian refugees, Wausau is now home to Chinese, Cambodians, Filipinos, Norwegians, Albanians, and a recent influx from the former Soviet Union and Eastern Bloc nations. Wausau and hundreds of communities of all sizes are experiencing significant changes in their populations (Wausau, Wisconsin, Web site).

Of course, this dichotomy of perception about community is what makes the journey interesting. There is a demographic mosaic that can be learned from and embraced. John Gardner's challenge for the demographic diversity of our communities has never been more important. He said that we must create "wholeness out of diversity," that is, embrace our differences as well as our commonality (Gardner, 1990, p. 116). The nation is evolving demographically. With this change comes new challenges and opportunities to make decisions and implement strategies that create communities that welcome, support, and sustain newcomers.

Assimilating new people into communities presents challenges and opportunities. Some longtime residents are concerned that the newly settled groups will overburden schools, services, and employment. In areas that are depressed economically, contenders for the few jobs available are resentful when more job seekers enter the pool. But this is just one side of the story and unfortunately the one we hear most about.

On the other side of the story are successful experiences that occur when the assimilation process and welcome mat work together. In the Fargo-Moorhead area, there is a conscious effort to create opportunities for foreign-born newcomers to assimilate into the community, with language programs, job counseling, and places to meet on issues and concerns. Through Cultural Resources, Inc., the region has created a structure to positively bridge the transition not only for the newcomers but also for longtime residents. In Wausau, Wisconsin, the school system has developed programs to help children and parents who are foreign-born have a positive school experience. As one school official said, "Our relationship and support of newcomers ultimately makes Wausau a more desirable place for business to locate and for people to live and raise families."

Finding Community Solutions from Within

Over the last several decades, many well-intentioned "solutions" have been applied to communities of all sizes. Whole blocks and neighborhoods have been demolished; whole blocks and neighborhoods have been built; waterfronts have been repaired; downtown cobblestones have been installed; downtown cobblestones have been removed; small-business investments have been made; large-business incentives have been given. You name it. Some of the many efforts have worked, but by and large the one-size-fits-all solutions have fallen short.

The methods for improving communities that have had the most success are those where nonprofits, business, local government, and citizens have made a commitment and an investment to make their particular situation better. Research has shown that when residents of low-income housing projects get invested, things get better. Evidence further suggests that what distinguishes safe neighborhoods from unsafe ones is not the ratio of police to residents or the frequency of probation offenses but rather the social fabric of the neighborhood and the condition of families (Annie E. Casey Foundation, 1999). When business takes an interest in the schools or when local government incorporates citizens into the decision-making process, things usually get better. Community success is not only possible, it is happening when communities come together.

For its major initiative, Wanted: Solutions for America, begun in 1998, the Pew Partnership looked across America for programs that were working. The research documented clearly that discrete approaches to community programs are achieving documentable results. Because the programs studied dealt with diverse issues, ranging from dental health for children, to reducing substance abuse among teens, to providing access to financial capital for low-income and underserved populations, it was the common threads that were of most importance to seek out. It became clear that solutions occur when connections are made between people and organizations and also between resources and needs. Results happen when minds and attitudes are changed about the problem, about the stakeholders, and about the communities themselves. Successful efforts solve problems on the scale that is called for. They define their scope and work in manageable pieces. Finally, the best program results occur when there is inclusion, participation, and deliberation (Freedman, 2003).

Community success must be measured block by block, neighborhood by neighborhood, and city by city. Despite the glimmers of hope that shine through, there are just as many community failures. The question, of course, is "Why some places and not others? Why some neighborhoods and not others?" Peirce and Guskind (1993) contend that relationship and civic engagement provide a key to the kind of success every community seeks: "Positive urban break-throughs rest not so much on electing brilliant people to office—though it is surely handy to have them there—as on the birth of a civic culture of cooperation and a belief in the future, with indi-viduals willing to take up the torch to make that better future a real-ity. . . ." (p. 3). Success then is not driven by one political party, a revitalized downtown, or even a new high school; it is about new ways of doing business, different ways of thinking about place and people. As Peirce and Guskind say, "The challenges in American society are far more complex than simply putting roofs over people's heads. They have to do with community" (p. 4). The empowerment of people in solving their own problems is *the* vehicle for civic change and must be the overriding factor as we seek to build and rebuild communities.

These ideas of community, citizen empowerment, and grassroots solutions square with the experiences of communities throughout the United States. We have all realized that Jane Jacobs (1961) was right that billions of dollars will not fix cities. However, what will and is "fixing" communities is their own capacity for change and the way they go about their collective work. How people in a com-munity see themselves and one another has everything to do with their well-being and that of their community. If they believe that change can happen, it usually does.

Harvard Professor Robert Putnam's study (1993, p. 36) of twenty Italian communities found that some were economically and socially prosperous whereas others were fractious and had a lower standard of living. The difference, he concluded, was the result of generations of building trust and goodwill through "networks of civic engagement"—choral societies, civic groups, newspaper read-ership—that has allowed some of the communities to work together on issues of importance. The more prosperous regions drew on large stores of social capital. Putnam and his colleagues contend that civic capacity is built when citizens take ownership and pride in their surroundings and interest in the well-being of people around them.

Cornelia Butler Flora and Jan L. Flora (1990, p. 8, pp. 197–207) observed this trend of "civic ownership" in their research on rural communities in the Great Plains and the West. Their research concentrated on how economic conditions have affected ranching and farming communities. They found that rural communities must retain more of the resources that they have traditionally exported, including bright, hardworking young people, and they must know how to work together if they are to remain viable through the current macroeconomic challenges. These observations of rural communities, Putnam's research on Italian communities and later on American communities, and Richard Florida's research on creative communities are further evidence that what happens *in* a community is as important as what happens *to* a community. The normal cyclical progression of economies, leaders, and the influence of outside factors affects every community at one time or another. Those that manage these inevitable changes are places that have developed a sense of the future that includes and is shared by the larger community.

New Ways of Working

The analysis and the solutions to problems for communities of all sizes will require a different approach. Focusing on the bounty, not the drought, is the key to both understanding and improving communities. In a 1992 conference on solutions for urban America, sponsored by three of the nation's larger foundations, Annie E. Casey, Ford, and Rockefeller, the tone of the conversation was a departure from the decades of "urban strategy" sessions. The discussions moved away from the more technical aspects of cities, like planning, municipal-bond options, and solid-waste disposal, to the more intangibles, like community building, engaging stakeholders, and tapping community assets. Recognizing that the large carrots of federal and state money were probably things of the past, participants proposed holistic approaches, which moved away from solution wars and identified practical steps that every community could use. The advice from this conference called for communities to have structures and vehicles for defining their vision of their future. Stable community-based organizations or development corporations (or both) must be in place and functioning. Diverse coalitions must be established that involve the stakeholders in and out of the affected area (or problem). This includes the need to develop leadership at all levels and encourage the empowerment of people to affect their own lives. Finally, communities seeking alliances and partnerships to revitalize communities must face persistent concerns about how to address race and ethnicity in an increasingly pluralistic society.

The focus for the future must be on how American communities *can* work and work better. Even though history has shown us lessons, directions, and examples of positive change, cities have been so bombarded by problems and challenges that there is little time, money, or sometimes even interest to take the long view. They have been pressured to do something and do it now. Expediency is one route to take, but community histories are fraught with the results of too much, too fast, too little, or too slow. The Three Bears had the winning combination: just right is what we need in the new community model. This new approach will take time, thought, and persistence.

Getting Started in Your Community

Community challenges took generations to take hold and may take generations to solve. The questions, of course, are these: How do you know what to do? and How do you know when to do it? There are day-to-day demands, unexpected expenditures, and inevitable changes because of weather, new demands, economic downturns, and competing choices. How can you ever know for sure?

The answers lie in the seven leverage points that frame this book: investing right the first time, working together, building on community strengths, practicing democracy, preserving the past, growing leaders, and inventing a brighter future. However, change of any kind requires that there be the desire for change, a willingness to do things differently, and a belief that a change of behavior or tactics will produce a different result. To begin this process, it is critical that you know your community better. Who lives in your community? What are the critical issues facing the community? What needs to happen for change to occur? Building on this foundation of knowledge, you can then begin to join with others to implement the processes in the chapters that follow. As a practical matter, you need some colleagues to join you. I suggest that you organize a brown-bag or even an e-mail chat with several other people to begin this process of change. Remember that the conversation in the community is different now—you are in it.

Communities are rich mosaics of size, people, institutions, traditions, even problems. The pieces fit together in a pattern, but pieces can be added that change the design entirely. For our purposes, the new pieces are the proven strategies for success that are found in the following seven leverage points. They broaden and enrich the notion of community for everyone. Change strategies really work only when they include all people in creating a new mosaic.

2

Investing Right the First Time

We must design our efforts for the long haul.
Short-term programs won't do it.

John Gardner

A few years ago on a visit to a city in the heartland of America, I got a great insight on community investments. On the table was a plan for a legitimate job-training program for former gang members. The idea was well designed and offered an alternative to the financial lures of the streets. At issue was the bottom line: it is expensive to offer job-training and work opportunities for individuals with limited formal education and in some cases criminal records. At one point during my visit, I said that the program seemed expensive, to which one of my hosts replied, "How much is your life worth?" The statement was simple and brief; the message powerful. We must do what must be done in our communities even if the price tag is high or the work hard. All of our lives, my colleague reminded me, are intrinsically linked. No longer do railroad tracks, competing high schools, or gated communities separate us. All of us are dependent on the well-being of others. In other words, invest now or pay later.

This exchange has stayed with me for over a decade. Our discussion was essentially about helping bright, capable young people reclaim their own lives. Ultimately, it was not a dollars-and-cents conversation. It had much more to do with our values and what is important to us as a community. Think about it in terms of risk management. Was I, as a potential funder, willing to "risk" that this group of young people would get themselves on the right track without this program or one like it? The circumstances were such that the risk of *not* investing was just too high for me. I made the financial commitment.

This has led me to think more about how we manage our community investments. The outcomes are no more certain than in the financial markets, but somehow we have not been willing to frame our priorities in terms of good investment strategies. In some instances, like early childhood education and parent education, we are almost ensured a great return. But even with very convincing evidence, we still believe that problems will just solve themselves. They won't.

Framing the Issues

This chapter develops the idea that communities need investment strategies, just as individuals do. In order to achieve results on major issues, we have to think more strategically about how to invest, where to invest, and when to invest. No longer can budgeting be done just incrementally; community resources must be strategically placed.

To illustrate the concept of community investing, I have selected a single issue—dropout prevention—set in two very different communities. The first community, Cedar Rapids, Iowa, has one of the lowest dropout rates in the nation. The school system has demonstrated the importance of investing in strategic ways to positively influence the decision by students to stay in school. The second example, the Dallas Independent School District, has one of the highest dropout rates in the nation. The district, however, has implemented some innovative solutions that are beginning to show positive results. The dropout issue is one of a myriad of issues requiring a clear investment strategy, as communities consider asset allocation, program priorities, and economic development. Statistics have shown that the long-term cost of a student dropping out of high school affects individual earnings, prevents the development of needed skills and competencies, and can create a significant financial burden in lost taxes and wages.

What will give the greatest return? What are the opportunity costs of not investing in a certain strategy? To ensure overall community well-being, how can the community portfolio be balanced? This chapter will address these questions. However, the answers will ultimately come from citizens, policymakers, business leaders, non-profit groups, and others in individual communities who create a community portfolio that is strategic and preemptive.

Understanding the Diversity of Investments

Albert Einstein once remarked that compound interest was the greatest discovery ever made. Likewise, interest that is generated on community investments can yield impressive results. Community investments can produce dividends for individuals as well as for the community over time. These investments keep on giving.

At first glance, the priority of community investments or budget allocations seems obvious. We should invest in human beings because we must have a trained and qualified workforce. End of conversation. Not so fast: communities built strictly around the fueling of the economic engine (at the exclusion of the supporting amenities and places for citizens to gather and interact) lose. A balanced approach to community investing pays attention to all parts of the community—the needs, the opportunities, and the amenities. How do you decide how much to spend on one over the other? Isn't it better to invest in the public schools or job training than in a new minor-league baseball park? There is no either-or answer: you must have a balanced community portfolio. Even if every person in the community who needed job training got it, attention must still be paid to the other kinds of investments needed to make a vibrant community. This begs very important questions: Is there a hierarchy of needs for community investments? Isn't it better to invest in the basics first before going off to do something else? If we can't feed people, do we really need another museum? These are all good questions and are often discussed in the city council chambers and in coffee shops. The critical consideration is not one over the other necessarily but rather an understanding of how the pieces fit together to make a strong community. There is no numerical formula. Certain kinds of investments are harder to measure than others. A job-training program that prepares people for better jobs, and thus higher wages and taxes, may take several years to yield a noticeable return. However it is fairly easy to count receipts from a new baseball stadium. The bottom line is that communities need to think about all kinds of investments and not be mesmerized by short-term returns nor stymied by long-term prospects. Robert McNulty makes a persuasive case for "amenities as urban investment" by claiming that those investments in parks and recreation, aquariums, and museums "instill a sense of place and a common purpose—two critical elements that are often missing in depressed areas" (1993, pp. 231–232).

Investment capital comes in a number of different forms. *Human capital* refers to investments in people directly, through job training or schooling, but also to secondary investments that enhance their ability to participate better in society. *Physical capital* is generally considered to be the infrastructure of a community, such as highways, power plants, and sewer systems. It can also include structures that we think of as development capital, such as affordable housing, sports stadiums, and civic centers. *Social capital* is built through the social networks that create norms of reciprocity and trust in a community (Putnam, 2000, p. 21). It includes memberships in civic clubs, religious organizations, and sports leagues. *Civic capital* refers to those places and institutions that bring people together. It can cross over other forms of capital, but generally these are investments in place, such as parks, cultural centers, and theaters.

There are other forms of capital, including *financial*, that provide access to dollars and the credit markets, particularly for the most disadvantaged. There is also *environmental capital*, which refers to a community's natural resources, including water, land, air, wildlife, and vegetation (Green and Haines, 2002, pp. 139–179). While all forms of capital must be considered, the primary focus of this chapter is human, physical, social, and civic capital.

Our understanding of capital investments takes on new meaning as we weigh the benefits of a variety of capital investments to the overall well-being of a community, its people, and its economy. Robert Putnam's groundbreaking book (1993) on Italian communities titled *Making Democracy Work: Civic Traditions in Modern Italy*, provided convincing evidence on the long-term benefits of large stores of social capital. What we are continuing to learn is the interrelationship between various forms of capital and the interchangeability of the forms with the purpose.

As Table 2.1 shows, certain forms of capital can be isolated around traditional definitions. Roads and bridges are clearly physical capital, but are libraries and schools? Certainly, these are buildings, but they have larger applications in the community. They can be safe meeting places for people; they can anchor a community in social and civic ways as well as educational ones; they can connect people in new ways. Public transportation connects people to jobs but also to each other.

The challenges in considering capital investments are twofold: first, a community must decide what kinds of investments it must make. This requires choices driven by necessity, desire, and public will. It might be necessary to repair a bridge with the money set aside for a new community center, for example. Public safety could demand the choice. Second, another perspective that is becoming clearer is that we have to think about how all our investments interrelate and support the overall goal of a stronger, more prosperous community. That is where the balanced community portfolio is important. Capital investments done wisely and strategically reinforce each

Table 2.1. Types of Community Investments

Human Capital	Social Capital	Civic Capital	Physical Capital
Public education	Athletic leagues	Museums	Roads and highways
Literacy programs	Volunteer centers	Parks	Historic buildings
Pre-K education	Community gardens	Theaters	Hotels
Job training	Block clubs	Community meeting rooms	Libraries
Alternative schools	Neighborhood associations	Festivals	Sewer, water, and power systems
Leadership training	Civic clubs	Parades	Civic centers
Health screening	Book clubs	Sports teams	Public transportation
English-as-a-second- language programs	School organizations	Arts programs	Bridges
	Religious affiliations	Concerts	Airports
Child care	Farmers' markets	Cultural centers	Parking facilities
Job fairs	Dance groups	Sidewalks*	Affordable housing
			Schools

Note: For an expanded discussion of these forms of community capital investments, see Green and Haines, 2002, pp. 81–100 (human capital); Putnam, 2000, pp. 22–28 (social capital); McNulty, 1993, pp. 231–249 (civic capital).

*The notion of sidewalks as civic and physical capital is attributable to Mayor Joseph Riley, Charleston, South Carolina.

other. They create a different scenario for the community. It is important to consider all the possibilities for a community investment strategy. Examples of the kinds of investments that communities must consider are wide ranging.

A community's investment strategy depends in part on its value system, its tolerance for risk, and its long-term vision: the same kinds of decisions that individuals must weigh in their personal-investment strategy. In addition, possible economic downturns must be considered. Very elaborate financial and community plans have been derailed by the economy. There can be significant opportunity costs, however, of *not* investing in certain areas. This requires that the community articulate a collective vision and know the options for investing that are available. For communities, it is not a choice between stocks or bonds, but rather investments in a range of programs and priorities. The returns on these investments are not always measured in financial terms but are evaluated by greater civic participation, greater human productivity, stronger families, more collaborative ways of working, and extensive social and civic networks. There are different ways to measure and leverage these capital assets as well as strategies to encourage new community investors. In other words, a community's investment strategy takes considerable time and talk before it is ready to implement.

Choosing the Right Investment

It would be nice if there were a community crystal ball to tell us what would be the best investment over the long run. Unfortunately, that luxury does not exist on Main Street or Wall Street. Communities have to rely on their ability to use common sense to make decisions based on equity and fairness; they have to draw on the knowledge and experience of others who have had success; and they have to start where they are. A listing of smart decisions made in the last century is not very helpful to those who have made plenty of bad decisions. It is helpful, however, to challenge ourselves to create a better process for decision making that gets us to the destination we want, to have a better alert system in place to pick up problems and opportunities, and to build a process to learn from failures and successes.

A community investment strategy can, and often does, rest with elected officials—those with the responsibility for the budget. However, citizens must have a say in how the funds are appropriated by asking questions, requesting data, and requiring that annual budgets be more than increments of past budgets. Likewise, schools, nonprofit agencies, and public-private ventures must all apply the same rigor to their own investing.

A social investment strategy is a different mind-set. Although there is always demand to first be included in a budget and then to get more, investing requires that citizens and others think about long-term implications of certain kinds of decisions. Not every demand in the budget process is equal; some programs or initiatives are critical to the long-term health of the community. Issues such as early childhood education, public health, and school success must be considered as priority items that could result in significant impact. The level of the investment should match the seriousness of the issue, the ability to affect the issue long term, and the potential impact on the community. Questions that citizens, organizations, and government should be asking are these: Are we funding stopgap measures or long-term solutions? Are we preventing or reacting? What are the results of past investments in specific issues?

Communities are faced with a multitude of decisions on ways to develop, issues to address, and solutions to seek. The underlying question in most discussions and deliberations is this: Which direction is best? Of course, there are no sure and fast rules for making community decisions. There are several things that help influence the community decision-making process. The first is information. As more accurate information becomes available, it helps sort out the immediacy of an issue. Communities get behind the solution and begin to create strategies to address the issue when they understand the seriousness of the problem and understand what must be done to solve it. The second extenuating factor is timing (sometimes an issue deserves immediate attention)—that is, the community must act now or lose the opportunity. Examples of this include an opportunity to lure a high-wage facility to the area; a decision on annexation; or as will be discussed in Chapter Six, the preservation of land, buildings, or landmarks. This level of decision making certainly draws strength from thorough information and timely action but often, and more important, it depends on the community's collective value system: What is important to us?

Getting People to Focus on Issues

Deciding to invest in a community issue or opportunity is not automatic no matter the importance. Issues make their way into the public's psyche in several stages. The issue attention cycle goes from latent concern, to the public agenda, and then to the policy agenda (Luke, 1998; Downs, 1972; Coates, 1991). However, as in most things "public," the sequencing of steps or events is often unpredictable. Focus on the issue is lost or gained depending on other external circumstances and the resonance of the issue to the public's perception of overall well-being. It is hard to get attention focused on anything unless the public connects personally in some way. There is a general cycle of concern that accompanies issues and brings them to the forefront of the public's and the policymakers' attention. Further, the public's attention can be diverted temporarily by a war, a human tragedy, a natural disaster, or even a high-profile trial or criminal pursuit. In the summer of 2003, there were several serious weather stories in different parts of the country—wildfires in the West and storms in the South. Reporting at the national level was sparse even though lives and livelihoods were threatened. This happened to occur at the same time that Saddam Hussein's sons were reported killed. Attention was deflected.

In a general sense, awareness and visibility of issues occurs in several ways. Information that clearly describes a problem alerts people. Citizens and the media tell stories and people listen. Trend data (things are getting worse) or comparison data (our community is worse than another) also raise attention. For example, in the early nineties, a midwestern newspaper ran a series of articles that showed the community's teen pregnancy rates as some of the highest in the nation. The community woke up and began to take action. In order to get the public's attention, the situation has to have real and personal qualities. It is not enough to read about numbers of people; it is also important to see and hear about the effects on a real person. Even more attention is paid if people see the situation in terms of their own family: "It could be my child." News stories about a bright, capable young person gunned down for no apparent reason or interviews with young people who are planning their own funerals make citizens take notice. Emotional investment in an issue is a powerful motivator. When people read or hear about a particularly outrageous situation "that just shouldn't have happened," they connect. There must also be a sense that something can be done about the issue, that impact can be made. It is important for people to feel that remedies are possible through investing and acting. Issues move from a condition (an existing situation or latent problem), to a problem (an issue that captures the public's attention and the headlines), to a priority (a situation that requires action by either the public or decision makers to prevent a worsening of the situation). Community issues become policy concerns when they can move up on the policy agenda, usually displacing something else (Luke, 1998, pp. 41–54).

Issues with Currency

As we have seen, two factors that influence a good community investment strategy are information and timing. I have singled out one particular issue, school dropouts, as representative of the importance of those factors and their application in real-life community decisions. School dropout is precisely the kind of issue where more accurate information on the causes, on the remedies, and on the problem itself could help inform how the public thinks about the issue and about the urgency of solving it. The timing of an investment in preventing school dropouts is crucial, because the window of opportunity may be quite small. Waiting until a child is in high school may be too late.

Perhaps the greatest example of human capital investment is education. Debates rage in state houses, Congress, and in the White House about standards of learning, teacher pay, and equity funding, to name just a few. Within this complex and sometimes polarizing conversation, however, is the realization that we are leaving some children behind *forever*. Staying in school—high school—is critical to the long-term financial and personal success of a student and the community. Postsecondary education increases earning power and job flexibility, but a high school diploma is a necessity for the first rung on the economic ladder. In two recent assessments of outcomes for children, youth, and families, both the Annie E. Casey Foundation *Kids Count 2002 Data Book* (2002) and Save the Children's *America's Forgotten Children* (2002) cited staying in school as a major factor in achieving self-sufficiency in urban and rural areas. As Casey Foundation president Douglas Nelson writes, "Success in today's economy requires more education than ever before yet millions of working parents are high school dropouts" (p. 11). Or in the case of rural America, "Finishing high school and going to college do not seem to be realistic goals" (Save the Children, 2002, p. 77).

There is little argument that staying *in* is better than dropping out—but how much better? For the one million young people who dropped out of school between October 1999 and October 2000 and joined the ranks of literally millions more who have made the same decision, they can expect a lifetime of lower earnings. According to the 2000 U.S. census, a high school dropout twenty-five years of age or older can expect to earn a median annual income of $21,400 versus $28,800 for a high school graduate. In the United States, approximately 18 percent of the population over the age of twenty-five does not have a high school diploma. The percentages range from Mississippi, with 25.4 percent, to Alaska, with 10.4 percent (U.S. Bureau of the Census, 2002; revised September 4, 2003).

If the dropout story ended with the individual, it would be bad enough, but the lifetime implications for the individual's family and for society are equally significant. Children from poor families are more likely to drop out. Further, children from families with low levels of educational attainment are at greater risk of dropping out (Kaufman and others, 1996). But the most shocking statistic is directed toward society at large: each year's cohort group of youth who do not finish high school will cost the nation $260 billion in lost earnings and foregone taxes over their lifetime (Burt, 1998, p. 30). For individuals, their families, and our society, we must invest in ways to keep young people in school and reclaim those who have left.

The school dropout issue provides an excellent example of the importance of timing investment decisions. Because the investment is time sensitive—as early as first grade according to some researchers—every day counts. Even if the window is narrowed to perhaps the most vulnerable time for dropping out—ninth grade—the investment period comes and goes quickly. Although students are sometimes "reclaimed" by school systems, going back is harder than dropping out. The greatest return comes when young people stay in school.

Where to Invest

The public can care all it wants, but unless there is a sense of urgency and immediacy, the issue may linger toward the bottom of the policy agenda. Why? First, the dropout problem is perceived to affect a relatively small percentage of the total public school population. There is a general feeling that the focus in schools (and the resources) must be on those who *are* in school and plan to stay. Further, often the public at large and even school officials don't know the extent of the problem. Rates are hard to calculate, as students drop in and out of a system, families move, and lives change. According to researcher Phillip Kaufman (2001), there are real discrepancies in the ways that dropout rates are determined. He believes that the current practices of data collection are woefully inaccurate, with major discrepancies reported by local, state, and federal education agencies. He found different methods of data collection on target populations from the Bureau of the Census's Current Populations Survey (CPS), the National Center for Education Statistics Longitudinal Studies Program (NELS), and the National Center for Education Statistics common core of data (CCD). These differences in reporting lead to an underrepresentation of minority students in data sampling, which leads to large-scale bias in NELS and CCD and thus underestimates minority dropout levels (Harvard University, 2001).

The U.S. Department of Education (2001) has designated three ways to measure dropouts: event dropout rates, status dropout rates, and high school completion rates. All three are discussed here, but the National Center for Dropout Prevention recommends the status rate as the most accurate.

> *Status dropout rates* measure the number of 10th through 12th graders who leave school each year without receiving a diploma. According to the Department of Education report, somewhere between one-third and one-half a *million* young people did not complete high school in each year between 1990 and 2000 (347,000 to 544,000). The status rates tend to be larger than event numbers because they represent the proportion of young people ages 16 through 24 who are not in school and who have not earned a high school diploma. In October 2000, these young people represented 11 percent of the 34.6 million 16- to 24-year-olds in the United States, or almost four million individuals.

Event dropout rates measure the proportion of youth ages 15 to 24 who dropped out of high school in the preceding twelve months. In the most recent Department of Education report, *Dropout Rates in the United States 2000,* this percentage was five percent of the total high school enrollment of these age cohorts. This percentage decreased from 1972 to 1987 but has remained constant since then.

High school completion rates measure the proportion of 18- through 24-year-olds not currently enrolled in high school or below, who have completed a high school diploma or an equivalent credential such as the GED (General Education Development certificate). These numbers are different from the strict graduation rate. In 2000, 87 percent of all 18- through 24-year-olds not enrolled in high school had completed high school.

Even using the status rate, which gives a more complete picture of the severity of the problem in a particular system, the situation is still complicated because of the uneven data collection and varying definitions. Some have suggested that the problem of undercounting goes beyond methodology to pressures put on school systems to perform. If too many students drop out, that's a problem; if too many stay in school and fail the standardized tests, then that's a problem, too. Despite the arguments on how, and whom, to count or outside pressures, the numbers are staggering: approximately four million students between sixteen and twenty-four aren't in school and do not have a diploma. Even if some reenroll, the implications are profound for the long term. The situation, however, is not hopeless or irreversible.

Considerable research is needed on who drops out and why, but we do know where a significant number of these students live. In a study done for Harvard University's Civil Rights Project in 2001, researchers found that the national dropout problem is most severe in several hundred schools in the thirty-five largest cities in the United States. In these schools, less than 50 percent of the freshman class ever graduate. The report concludes what others have suspected for years: federal data on high school dropouts underestimate the number (Balfanz and Legster, 2001).

The good news is that something can be done and is being done. Amid the gloom and doom, many of these young people who have dropped out or who might drop out can have a brighter future if communities act—and act now. Will Jordan and James McPartland of Johns Hopkins University (1994) have identified three components of successful dropout programs that when in place reduce the occurrence of students dropping out before graduation. Parents, school administrators, and community leaders should use these components as an initial screen for evaluating efforts in their own communities.

1. Does your school system have smaller organizational structures within a school that assist students who are most likely to drop out?

2. Is there a core curriculum of high standards that allows students to recover from failure without the risk of retention?

3. Are teachers supported with professional-development opportunities by department? Do they have scheduled planning time?

McPartland and Jordan contend that a comprehensive set of specific changes that addressed these three areas could retain most of the current dropouts and help each student succeed in a high-standards program of study while enjoying school.

These remedies correlate with the reasons students say they drop out and what research has shown. There are no real changes in causes over the last couple of decades. Certain factors that tend to increase the likelihood of dropping out are these: not moving to the next grade, poor academic performance, and lack of interest in school and school activities (and feeling as if the school has no interest in them). Further, students who have parents with limited schooling (or unsuccessful experiences), who have behavior problems, who have trouble with the police, and who exhibit psychological vulnerability are more likely to drop out of high school than their peers who do not have these characteristics (Janosz, Le Blanc, Boulerice, and Temblay, 1997).

Investing for the Long Haul

Two cities—Cedar Rapids, Iowa, and Dallas, Texas—are taking innovative, inclusive looks at how they address the dropout rates and the key investments to stop the flow. These communities have very different challenges, but they are both making headway on the problem. Iowa has the third lowest dropout rate in the nation. In Cedar Rapids, there is clear evidence that the secret to success is in program flexibility, public awareness, resources, and commitment from the top of the educational hierarchy, which makes it possible and desirable for students to stay in school.

Dallas is a much bigger city, with one of the worst dropout rates in the nation. However, a set of investment decisions and determined leadership are showing early positive results. What is important about profiling two very different communities at different success points is to illustrate the connections in program approach, to understand better how challenges are being addressed, and to consider the decisions that must be made *now* to address the problem. Citizens, legislatures, parents, and elected officials should know the status of the investments and the decision making required in their community. It is never too late to make smart decisions.

Cedar Rapids: A Community Issue That Came to School

Located in eastern Iowa, the Cedar Rapids–Iowa City corridor was one of the fastest growing areas in all of Iowa in the eighties. With this growth, however, came a stark reality that there was a growing problem that could affect that prosperity: far too many young people were not reaching their potential and realizing the rewards that school success brings. In 1984, a decision by the state legislature to allow school districts to use a portion of general property tax revenue funds for programs to reclaim dropouts has made a significant difference. Four years later, the legislature allowed those funds to be used for dropout prevention also. The legislation designated that the amount available to each district was to be based on the percentage of district enrollment identified as returning dropouts and potential dropouts (which must not exceed 5 percent) and the district cost per pupil.

The Iowa Department of Education accepts applications from districts for funds that provide 75 percent of the program costs, with the other 25 percent coming from district funds. Moneys can be used in kindergarten through twelfth grade to establish programs, hire additional staff, and so forth. Ray Morley, consultant within Iowa's Bureau of Instructional Services regarding Homeless Children and Youth and At-Risk Student issues, said that the decision to tap into these funds is made at the local level by superintendents, business managers, and boards of education. Although the districts' requests must be approved by the Department of Education and the governor's office, the funding stream itself comes from local property taxes—from the taxpayers themselves. Morley believes that "built-in responsibility" and decision making at the local level increase the stake that the district has in working with the local and state collaborators: "If you have trust developed at the local level between staff, students, families, and communities, incredible things can happen." Happen they did in Cedar Rapids.

It was this consistent funding stream that was the impetus for Cedar Rapids to develop its dropout prevention programming and a direct reason for their success. The district was on the cusp of a potentially big problem, and they decided to take advantage of the funds available. The community was a pioneer in the alternative high school concept, with its Metro High School, established fifteen years ago with sixty students, now with six hundred. Alternative schools are designed to meet the needs of specific populations of students, such as gifted and talented, at risk, and special education, according to the City of New York Department of Education. Iowa was one of the first states in the country to implement this idea. Since the early seventies, Iowa's dropout rate has gone from 9 percent or more to under 1 percent.

Several things stand out about the Cedar Rapids system and the decisions they have made to improve retention. First, as a school system, they want to learn and improve. Administrators, teachers, and parents want accurate information on the problem and the results. Programs are evaluated externally; they ask the hard questions and they fix what is broken. For example, in 2002, the district knew it needed more information and began a yearlong evaluation of the middle school at-risk programs to assess three things: first, customer satisfaction—vehicles to ask students, parents, and teachers whether the programs are meeting their needs; second, a typology of best-practice components from the system and other research and practice; and third, determined outcome or research measures. In brief, the system is asking itself three key questions: Do we have programs that are effectively meeting academic and social needs? What is the best available knowledge in the design and delivery of these programs? And are we making a difference, and if so, how and how much? Every school system in America should be asking and answering questions just like these.

Early findings from this research suggest that aggressive outreach programs tend to have better results in Cedar Rapids and elsewhere. According to Jane Caraway, program facilitator in the Office of School Leadership, Cedar Rapids Community School District, the district is very proactive. In essence, Cedar Rapids does whatever it takes to keep kids in school. This involves teachers actually visiting the child's home to find out about the absenteeism. This approach seems to have the highest results. According to Caraway, this approach targets the 10 to 15 percent of children that nothing seems to touch because they don't come through the door. Having teachers and administrators personally involved with keeping kids in school is one of the key factors in their success.

Cedar Rapids not only identified the problem early and decided to change the trend immediately, but they are also creating a learning environment to get better at what they are doing. Rather than hide or doctor the statistics, they want to know results. Their comparative results present a hopeful picture and a guide for others to follow.

Dallas: Making It Hard for Students to Give Up

The second largest city in Texas, Dallas has one of the nation's largest and most diverse school systems. Among its 164,000 students, 58 percent are Hispanic, 34 percent African American, 7 percent white, and 1 percent other races. More than three-quarters of Dallas public school children receive free or reduced-price lunch, and almost a third of the pupils have limited English proficiency. The state of Texas was ranked in the lowest quartile in the nation in 1999 in high school dropout rates. The state's largest cities—Austin, Dallas, Houston, and San Antonio—are in the pool of the thirty-five school districts that have the worst national rates (Balfanz and Legster, 2001). In a state that is looking for answers to stem the dropout rates, Dallas is asking the right questions and mobilizing the right agencies and organizations to find them.

A key decision for Texas started in 1984 when the state legislature passed HB 72, which mandated sweeping reforms in the state's public education system, including several aspects of the dropout issue. Part of the legislation included authorization for the Texas Education Association to implement a system for collecting data on student dropouts and the beginning of efforts to reduce the dropout rate to no more than 5 percent. This was followed in 1987 and 1989 with legislation that substantially increased state and local responsibilities for collecting student dropout information, monitoring dropout rates, and providing dropout prevention services. In the latter bill, districts exceeding the state dropout target would be required to allocate a percentage of the compensatory education funds to remedial and support progress for at-risk students the following year. These legislative actions have affected the outcomes

for the last fifteen years or so in several ways. Prior to this legislation, districts could collect or not collect data at their discretion.
The new reporting requirement brought the issue of dropouts to the
attention of the school personnel, the state legislature, the media,
and the public. The state's largest newspapers ran front-page stories
about the problem. Finally, it was on the radar screen.

It is with these state mandates that the Dallas Independent
School District assessed its progress. Things were improving but not
improving enough from the standpoint of Mike Moses, who became
superintendent of schools in January 2001. "Kids drop out when
they don't have any hope," says Moses. "We are trying to make it
hard for them to give up," but too many are giving up. Twenty-five
percent of all ninth-grade students districtwide are not moving on
to tenth grade because they do not have enough credits. This is
a critical period in the dropout decision timetable. The district
has launched an internal and external campaign to change not only
the numbers but also the negative odds for thousands of kids in the
system in the ninth-grade level and below. The district wants not
only to keep students in school but also to bring them back. They
are attacking the problem on all fronts. On the recovery side, they
initiated *reconnection centers* in 1999 to provide a nonthreatening
place with up-to-date curricula for students who want to come back.
Young people go to computer labs and do much of their course work
online, with a teacher doing the testing and the grading. Almost
six thousand students are currently enrolled in these recovery
programs—students who had dropped out or were likely to. This
approach gets students who are beyond elementary or middle school
into a setting where they can reconnect to education. Many of the
local community colleges are equipped with the curricula software,
so students can go to those locations on the weekends. H. B. Bell,
associate superintendent for Alternative Programs, reports that
more than a thousand students graduated through this program in
2002, and another fifteen hundred are expected to graduate in 2003.
If national calculations are correct, the district just increased the
earnings of those students by almost $3 million dollars over their

lifetime and added much-needed revenue to the coffers of the national and state tax collectors.

Even though the recovery efforts are impressive, Dallas understands that keeping kids in school is more cost-effective and more successful than trying to get them back in the system. Therefore more careful attention must be paid to the students *before* they drop out. Moses has challenged all the chambers of commerce in the area and other groups to join in mentoring a child. Rene Martinez, special assistant to the Superintendent for Dropout Prevention and Community Outreach, describes the program as a model mentoring program, targeting ninth-graders with standards based on national research. Mentors are trained and screened by Big Brothers–Big Sisters. Currently, there are 150 mentors in thirteen schools, but the goal is 1,000 mentors for ninth-grade students. These mentors include students, peers, and adults. In addition, the school system wants to provide meaningful adult mentors for students in all grades. Research has shown that one of the reasons students give for dropping out of school is the absence of a caring adult in their lives. This is a gap that the school system hopes to fill. Also, Martinez says, too many children, their parents, and community members have a deficit mind-set about education. High school graduation and access to college or higher education have too often seemed like the impossible dream. This realization meant that the local colleges and universities had to get involved. In meetings with every college and university president in the area, Martinez received commitments from these institutions to offer more resources to area students to encourage, inform, and excite high school students and their parents about post-secondary education. The activities include field trips to campuses, SAT and ACT preparation courses, increased availability of scholarships and aid, and opportunities to understand the educational options and raise expectations.

In surveys with parents, the district also learned that parents wanted to know more about the instructional lives of their children. This resulted in the creation of *parent academies*, offered on Saturdays, to provide more information about state assessments, access to higher education, talented-and-gifted programs, and so forth. More than nine hundred parents attended at least one of the first three academies throughout the year. Seven academies are planned for 2003–2004.

Dropouts affect the whole community, says Moses. So the question becomes this: Will the older, majority population realize that it is in their interest to pay to support the education of the minority population? The answer may lie in the old reality of enlightened self-interest. "If the students in the Dallas Independent School District don't graduate and develop key skills, they won't be able to fill the high-skill, high-wage jobs that are needed, and this affects the whole community," says Moses, matter-of-factly. It is in everybody's interest to invest not only in the well-being of young people but also in the well-being of every aspect of the community—economic, social, and civic.

Dallas is a good example of a district that has rechanneled its efforts into smart decisions and investments that will affect the future. Their experience and that of most urban city districts is an uphill battle. Children are coming into the system less prepared and with obstacles of poverty and language proficiency that further hinder their progress. The district team has taken a realistic look at the school system and has begun to build partnerships with every stakeholder group, including students, to change the odds, not just beat the odds.

Lessons Learned: Investing Smart and for the Long Term

Both examples—Cedar Rapids and Dallas—illustrate many shared strategies and approaches. No longer are we in the dark about who is dropping out and why: we know. The difficulty is to catch the problem early, mobilize parents, and indeed whole communities to act and act fast. In addition, the standards and values set at the state level are key motivators for support and investment in local programs. Dropout prevention and dropout reclamation have to be deliberate and targeted priorities. It is not too late to start an *investment fund.* Communities must have clear objectives in mind. Citizens, parents, and nonparents need to ask the tough questions: What is the dropout rate in our community? Why do children say they are dropping out? What programs are in place to prevent dropping out? What can we do?

Getting Started in Your Community

For some reason, we don't like to talk of money devoted to education as an *investment.* We like to use terms like *the public good, the right of every child, the vehicle for democracy.* It is all this and more, but it is also an investment. We know what schooling means to the individual, the community, and the nation. We also know what not having it can mean. Education joins a whole host of issues, such as the environment, affordable housing, access to financial capital, health care, and job training, that are critical investment opportunities. The challenge is to figure out the priorities, build on investment strategy, and allocate the dollars. This idea of an investment strategy versus a budgeting strategy opens up a new way of thinking about long-term outcomes and the interrelationship of issues.

The first step in understanding the strategy is to determine how your community invests now. Who decides the priorities? What have been the "returns" or results on community investments? These questions should be directed first to local government about specific issues. For example, questions might be: What is the unemployment rate in the community? Is the problem a lack of jobs or lack of skilled workers? How much is the community investing in job training? Second, think about a strategy for addressing an issue such as living-wage jobs. What are the ways and the amounts your community invests to address these problems? Is it likely to generate interest or capital (financial and otherwise)? What are the costs of not investing? Just like any investor, people in a community need to know the answers to these questions: What are the costs? What are the options? What are the risks? Start asking those questions and looking for answers today.

3

Working Together

*We must define new relationships and better ways of
public decision making to forge trust between diverse
groups and to create an understanding that we are all
in this together.*

William Winter

Americans don't always agree. We have strong feelings about
athletic rivalries, political parties, and religious beliefs. There
is one thing, however, that receives almost universal agreement: working together is better. In a survey, What Will It Take:
Making Headway on Our Most Wrenching Problem, done by the Pew
Partnership for Civic Change in 2003, Americans overwhelmingly
(93 percent) said that working together more closely on community
problems leads to better results. When asked what would *most*
improve the quality of life in the community, 40 percent said working together versus 14 percent who said voting. These responses define
our challenge—how to make working together business as usual.

People join together on a myriad of projects, interests, and concerns. The nation has witnessed enormous outpourings of support
and generosity in times of crisis—floods, hurricanes, and tragedies
of all types. The evidence is clear that Americans can link arms and
join hands with the proper motivation. The key to community

success, however, is the *habit* of working together, not the *incident* of working together. Democracy itself hinges on the ability of citizens to hang together and hang tough on the critical issues of the day.

Framing the Issues

This chapter describes the processes and the motivation that support working together on issues of any magnitude. We no longer have the luxury of "going it alone." The complexity of the problems facing every community requires that people and organizations be willing and able to come together to craft strategies that are effective in good times and bad. In places where genuine joint action has occurred, results happen. These are not just "pie-in-the-sky" experiments, but rather gritty processes that bring citizens, educators, organizations, governments, and businesses together to create a different outcome. This chapter will look at the experiences of four communities—Chattanooga, Tennessee; Almena, Wisconsin; Austin, Texas; and Fargo, North Dakota—that have figured out that their collective futures are tied to their ability to define problems and opportunities and organize themselves to take action. Was it easy or always fun? Absolutely not, as they would tell you. It was a necessity.

Communities have the capacity to meet important challenges directly and multilaterally if they organize themselves to act. However, rarely is it just structure that is the key to success. In situations where businesses, local nonprofit organizations, citizens, and local government have worked together successfully, there have been some clear ground rules. John Pepper, former chairman and CEO of Procter & Gamble, contends that groups not only must have a purpose, a plan to make things happen, but also must build on the experience and work of others. He contends that successful community efforts start with a burning platform. "There needs to be an awareness in a community that a problem exists" (Pepper, 2002, p. 3).

Americans choose to work together in different ways and for different reasons. Sometimes it is sporadic and necessary because of an incident or circumstance. However, it is clear that sustained efforts—those developed for a purpose and that work over time—must have a structure for working together that has broad implications for building social capital, creating unusual partnerships, and taking action on systemic issues.

Problems Cannot Be Solved Alone

Community organizations of all sizes have found that deep-seated community issues cannot be solved by one group alone. This has come as a surprise to some communities that have "siloed," or narrowly conceived, their approaches to solutions. The seriousness of problems requires that groups recognize that most social problems are related, feed on one another, and cannot be addressed in isolation. For example, individuals who are making less than a living wage cannot afford decent housing in a safe neighborhood and cannot provide adequately for their children. The list goes on. Limited resources require that we use what we have in the best and most strategic ways. Sporadic interventions never solve systemic issues. The extent of our seemingly intractable problems, like childhood poverty, drugs, and lack of educational achievement, have caused community organizations, business, and government to reach across organizational lines to form new alliances out of necessity.

Community partnerships are motivated not only by self-interest but also by common interests. At the national level, it is not uncommon to see a broad range of organizations joining together on issues that affect their individual organizations in different ways. For example, the national debate on Americorps funding brought together a wide range of organizations and individuals that believed in the concept and felt that communities and the nation would suffer without the volunteers. Some of those people had a personal stake in the issue—their job or their agency depended on the appropriation; but others, although not personally affected, had seen the positive results in their community and wanted to register their concerns about funding cuts. It is important that community efforts of any magnitude include and seek not only the stakeholders who would logically be included but also some unusual partners.

In brief, stakeholders are those people and organizations who have an interest in changing a situation or an issue or in maintaining the status quo. They most often are individuals, groups, or organizations most affected by the causes or consequences of an issue or situation (Bryson and Crosby, 1992, p. 65). However, the most obvious stakeholders are not the only ones who have an interest and are valuable to the process. Two other groups are often overlooked: *knowledgeholders* and *ripple-effect stakeholders*.

Knowledgeholders

Knowledgeholders are people who have critical information about the issue but may not be directly affected by the issue or its consequences. They are different from "experts" in that their role is not to tell the group what to do but to assist the group in four ways:

1. Help group members present their concerns in more informed and precise ways

2. Increase access to information and level the playing field among stakeholders, some of whom may have greater positions of power

3. Raise controversial aspects of the issues that others may avoid

4. Help the group understand the systemic nature of the problem or opportunity and the interconnected parts

Knowledgeholders create a more coherent view of the situation, which is not influenced by individual interests, and offer new information that breaks the stereotypes and frames of reference from which problems are too often viewed. The result is that knowledgeholders can offer a new lens on the problem (Luke 1998, p. 70).

Ripple-Effect Stakeholders

Ripple-effect stakeholders represent individuals or groups that feel the second or third impacts of an issue. Often the immediacy of an issue draws only those most affected or those that have the greatest concern. A great example of ripple-effect stakeholders applies to global warming. At first glance, the interest groups would appear obvious: environmental groups, coastal property owners, businesses that produce chlorofluorocarbons, farmers, and manufacturers such as the auto industry and air-conditioning companies. One of the effects of global warming is that the temperature of the earth is increasing, causing changes in weather patterns and producing negative results in the form of floods, storms, and droughts. Therefore it is very important to include a new ripple-effect stakeholder in the global warming discussion: insurance companies. As one executive stated the case, global warming could "bankrupt the industry." It is certainly to their financial advantage to curb the causes of climate change that too often result in major property losses and human suffering (Luke, 1998, pp. 71–72).

The Need to Think Inclusively

All of this points to a need for communities to think broadly and inclusively as they come together to act on issues and opportunities that are important to their long-term future. As one person asked in a contentious community meeting, "Who do we need in this room to solve this problem?" This is a great guiding question on whom to invite.

The best answers to our most wrenching issues or glorious opportunities come when there is collective deliberation, judgment, and ideas. Communities can create powerful alternatives when these forces work together. There are several ways that the process of working together manifests itself. Sometimes it's informal—people just getting together to make something happen. More often than not, there are structures in place that allow a community to work more systematically toward common goals.

What Is Working Together?

I thought working together meant gathering a large group. I learned the difference in my early days with the Pew Partnership. During site visits to over thirty communities to decide on grantees, the veil was lifted on what it really means. For our first initiative, the Civic Change project, eligible communities were asked to select an issue that was of critical importance to the community and then include those who were most relevant to solving the issue so they could collaborate on the proposal and then on the project, if selected. As a way to streamline the visits to the thirty finalist communities, the guiding principle for the site visits was a half-day meeting for the collaborative group—no subgroups, splinter committees, or private appointments. This seemed like a great idea until I realized on one of my early visits that hardly anyone in a room of twenty-five people actually knew one another very well at all, though they were "collaborating" on the proposed project. Lesson number one about working together is this: never assume that a large group gathered means that the individuals have worked together, will work together, or even might work together for any reason. Breakfast meetings with an outside visitor can usually draw a crowd, but assume nothing until you have a better read on their relationship.

This one experience caused me to begin to ask what working together really meant. Words like *collaboration* and *partnership* were cast about regularly, but did they mean more than a casual meeting or conversation? For me, working together is the ability of a group of people to develop a relationship of trust that will allow different perspectives to be heard and discussed but with ultimate agreement to take action. That's more than a breakfast meeting. Joining together requires trust and relationships as well as process and information. Citizens joining together in common action is never an abstraction. What *might* work or *could* work *only* works when people actually do something together.

The spectrum of working together usually includes some version of *partnerships, coalition building,* and *collaboration.*

Partnerships

Partnerships are common community structures formed between individuals, organizations, government agencies, and businesses that want to combine forces for results that match their own organization's best interests. In a survey done in 2001, *In It for the Long Haul: Community Partnerships Making a Difference*, by the Pew Partnership for Civic Change (2001a) with business, government, and nonprofit leaders in the two hundred largest cities, respondents cited a number of payoffs for partnerships beyond just the organizations involved or the specific issue addressed by the partnership.

1. Community partnerships raise visibility on local issues: it's hard for communities to solve problems they don't know about.
2. Partnerships can help communities set priorities for the allocation of resources.
3. Partnerships can unleash new talents and resources to address old and new problems and opportunities.

According to these leaders, partnership activities include information sharing and financial and in-kind support, but the critical function is tackling tough issues together. This was seen by leaders in all sectors as essential to community success. Almost three-quarters of the business and nonprofit leaders and 90 percent of the government leaders said that they work with other groups in the community to address important issues. Although the partnerships take different forms and directions, the survey found that they are clearly forged around key issues. Specifically, nonprofit, government, and business leaders say that they communicate with different sectors on a regular basis; they provide direct services to community organizations beyond giving and create a *culture of caring* within their respective organizations; more than 50 percent of businesses and 40 percent of local governments give employees paid time off to volunteer; and finally, all sectors say that they organize employee participation programs to help in the community through walk-a-thons, food drives, and so forth. Further, a clear majority serve on boards and invite representatives from the other sectors to serve on these boards. Partnerships, according to these executives, are alive and well and making a significant difference in the life of the community.

Coalition Building

A second type of joint work strategy is coalition building. Coalitions can be informal or formal arrangements that bring diverse groups together for joint action on a single issue or a set of issues. Members may have very different motivations for joining the coalition. Coalitions can be short term or long term, but throughout members retain their individual identities, goals, and missions Coalitions are formed for joint action to advocate to stop something or to start something. We have seen groups gather around traffic, crime, smoking, economic development—you name it.

Collaboration

The third type of community structure falls under a broad category called collaboration. Collaboration means simply "to work together," but its larger definition has a clear set of requirements and assignments (Chrislip and Larson, 1994, p. 5). Both a process and a goal for community work, collaboration allows multiple stakeholders in a community to work together toward a common purpose, building on the community's resources, talents, and assets. Understandably, this basic definition is the first step in the journey. All too often, communities declare that this initiative or that is a collaboration; it rarely is at first glance. Collaboration is more often talked about than actually done! It is one of the hardest community efforts to organize and execute but can be the most effective. It is difficult for groups and individuals to "give up" the control necessary to form a genuine collaboration. With the shortage of funds, too many only want their light to shine.

Collaboration is really one in a family of joint efforts that include *networking, coordination*, and *cooperation*. A collaborative relationship evolves, moves through stages, backs up, and moves again. As Cathy Jordan, formerly executive director of the McLennan County Youth Collaborative–Communities in Schools, Inc., in Waco, Texas, now at the Southwest Regional Education Laboratory, says, "When we created the collaboration [in Waco], we thought our work would be linear, moving ultimately to textbook definitions of collaboration. However, with changes in players and priorities, what evolved is a dynamic process of joint work that looks at times like a coalition and at other times like a true collaboration" (Morse, 1996, p. 8). The process, and the term for it, has been used to describe any event or set of events when community groups get together on an issue.

The continuum includes networking, which in brief includes information sharing about programs and interests; coordination, which requires that organizations exchange information and alter activities for mutual benefit; and cooperation, which requires information sharing, altering activities, the sharing of resources, and a commitment of time, the willingness to trust, and significant access to each other's turf (Himmelman, 2002, pp. 2–3).

Collaboration is the final step in the joint work continuum. Collaborations have certain criteria and standards that require that organizations alter their current activities, often create a new operating structure, and always share risks and rewards.

To say it another way, working together on collaboration requires new kinds of relationships. These can be characterized as much by the differences among the parties as by the similarities. When formed, these new relationships are powerful forces for change that could never be achieved by one organization working alone. New skills, new perspectives, and new people create new possibilities. If collaborations are viewed as new *constellations of stars* rather than as an effort to consolidate, downsize, or eliminate existing organizations or initiatives, then the value they can bring to a community—its issues and opportunities—is immeasurable.

Stages of Community Work

Creating venues for joint work is not a one-size-fits-all endeavor. Certain circumstances require different methods of working together. Table 3.1 shows the stages of collaborative community work. Community efforts of any description work if, and only if, there is a sense that they will accomplish something bigger than the collective parts and if the parties involved and those in the larger community think the process is fair and inclusive.

How Community Efforts Can Work Better

Community processes have characteristics all their own, but generally there are three phases that groups must address: *defining the problem*, *deciding on strategy*, and *taking action*. These are rarely linear and are not easy to predict in terms of time, or distinct blocks (Gray, 1989, p. 5).

Problem definition requires that the group come to agreement on the problem or the opportunity that they are addressing. This "cards-on-the-table" stage is the critical period where relationships and trust are built and ways of working agreed on. Other stakeholders are identified. It is critical that this early work create a clear view of the "big picture" and the commitment required. The second stage includes data gathering, goal setting, and overall organization of the process: how it will work, who will do what, the expectations both from and of members, and how the group will proceed. Finally, the group has to act. This stage can cause groups the most consternation because it requires moving from talk to action. This period could require a different structure or a change in the working group. A new group or subcommittee may be charged with monitoring the progress and the process. Gray's phases have three clear messages: pay attention to process; involve and communicate with a broad range of stakeholders; and be clear up front about expectations and commitments (Gray, 1989, pp. 86, 88–89).

Table 3.1. Assessing the Readiness for Joint Work

Networking	Coordination	Cooperation	Collaboration
Information exchange	Information exchange	Information exchange	Information exchange
	Authority retained by parties	Authority defined by parties	Shared authority, risk, resources, and responsibility
	Some planning or discussion of roles takes place	Significant planning and discussion of roles takes place	Comprehensive strategic planning
	Regular communication among parties	Regular communication among parties	Clear communication channels
		Access to one another's turf and span of responsibility	Alteration of current activities
			Noncompetitive environment
			Creation of new structure for operation
Goal: more knowledge of existing activities	*Goal: better efficiency in a particular task*	*Goal: better organizational performance*	*Goal: achievement of common purpose or mission*

Commitments of Time-Trust-Access

Note: This chart draws on the work of Arthur T. Himmelman's "Communities Working Collaboratively for Change," in *Resolving Conflict: Strategies for Local Government*, Margaret Herrman, ed. Washington, D.C.: International City/County Management Association, 1994, pp. 27–47.

Too many community efforts fail or never get off the ground because of several very familiar reasons. Perhaps the one best known is *turf*. People are afraid to join in, let go, and commit to activities over which they have limited control. Organizations often want to maintain their independence and keep their profile and good works high on the community's funding agenda. Joint work does not relieve an organization of its individual responsibilities or authority, but it does often create structures where the ultimate goal is a problem to be solved, not organizational survival. These efforts provide opportunities for people in jobs, agencies, and neighborhood groups to rethink how their organizational boundaries overlap and how they might be expanded to accomplish even more. Turf becomes less important as sustainable outcomes, economic vitality, and results take its place.

A second reason community efforts fail is that the fault lines of race, gender, socioeconomic difference, and age are issues that divide communities. All too often, fault lines define the dynamics of any community effort. Community groups must know this, deal with it as a group, and move on. Although years of injustice or exclusion cannot be ignored, the new effort can build a forum and an opportunity for people from throughout the community to build trust, form relationships, and focus on issues of common concern. An example of this process in action took place at a community forum on youth violence in a small city. The discussion was held on the campus of a historically black college. As various participants began to speak about their fears and concerns for their children, the color dividers came down. It was clear from the discussion and exchange that everybody in the room was concerned about the safety of all young people; the concern was color-blind. The issue was about children—all children—not one race or the other.

A third barrier to working together is the "been there, done that, won't work" mentality that exists everywhere. It is particularly prevalent if a community has had a history of false starts or setbacks on prior collaborative ventures. In those cases, it is important to step back, know the pitfalls, and hear the various opinions on the cause. A community must build on the knowledge of prior efforts but not be strangled by them. Also it is likely that the big issues in a community have been big issues for a while. It is also likely that there have been (or may currently be) ongoing efforts. With overlap almost ensured from one effort to another, groups must not only address the similarity but also acknowledge the new approach and the new people—the *what* and *who* that are making this effort different.

Community efforts are supported greatly by a community structure for change. This must be a stable but fluid organizing structure that allows the joint work to go forward, that provides supports and vehicles for getting new people involved, and that provides a system of accountability. Usually, these organizations operate with paid staff, volunteers, and an advisory group or board.

Finally, groups must be willing to spend ample time on the process of working together. When high energy "can-do" people get in the same room, there is a tendency and considerable pressure to "just do something." Too-quick responses can be fraught with mistakes and missteps. No one is suggesting indefinite discussion, but there is a need for a structure to help groups define issues and their various solutions before leaping to a particular remedy.

Working Together Is a Necessity, Not a Luxury

A clear message from research and practice is that working together is not optional anymore. As demands for services exceed available resources, we must think of ways to maximize time, money, and effort. Working together is one of the most effective ways to do it. We all like to think that we can do this or that alone. The reality is that the issues we must address, like affordable housing, living-wage jobs, and healthy families, require that we join forces. Getting a man on the moon required teamwork, an integration of knowledge, an investment of resources, and a clear vision of the goal. We should accept no less in our community work.

Community efforts like partnership, coalitions, and collaboration allow organizations and whole communities the opportunity
to imagine different options, think outside traditional lines, and get
more done. "The ultimate achievement for a collaboration is not
that it worked well among the collaborators, although that is highly
desired. Rather, it is that outcomes beneficial to a community are
brought about" (Council on Foundations, 1995, p. 9).

Communities and organizations will encounter predictable rough
spots, setbacks, and problems as they work together. However, amid
the need to tidy the process, establish norms, and ensure accountability from all the parties, it is important to realize that community
endeavors are not technical processes—they are, first and foremost,
human endeavors. They are also democratic practices—challenged
by the choices that must be made and the actions taken.

Wynton Marsalis provides a metaphorical framework for understanding the challenges and opportunities of working together in his
description of jazz. "Jazz is the music of conversation," says Marsalis,
and that is what you need in a democracy. A truly American art
form, jazz has its roots in homes, clubs, churches, and communities.
Modern-day jazz has evolved from pick-up music to a clear set of
sounds and styles. Marsalis describes jazz as a social invention. There
are clear parallels between his description of jazz and understanding
how communities do their work (Scherman, 1996, pp. 29–36).

Marsalis says that jazz must have attributes of music *and* other
things. There must be a willingness to play with a theme or concept, for example. In community language, it is the time when a
problem or opportunity is defined. Jazz invites participation and
reaction; so do collaboration and partnership. Third, jazz has an
inherent respect for individuality. "Playing jazz," says Marsalis,
"means learning how to reconcile differences, even when they're
opposites. . . . Jazz teaches you how to have dialogue with integrity"
(Scherman, 1996, p. 29).

The process of working together across sectors must encompass
human qualities as well as strategic ones. The jazz metaphor provides a straightforward preview of what can be expected and what

groups must do. The ability to work together comes when citizens realize for themselves that working together is not only better, it's the only real option for creating change.

The issues facing the four cities profiled in this chapter were different but sufficiently big and complex enough that they knew they needed more people and more organizations involved. In Chattanooga, the original idea of bringing people together evolved from a declining economic base, an environmental challenge, and a realization that something had to change or the results were going to be the same. Likewise in Almena, parts of the town were disappearing. The grocery store and the largest employer were already gone, and some were afraid that those losses were just the beginning of further economic and community decline. Austin was able to seize a big opportunity in the eighties because groups from throughout the community came together. In Fargo-Moorhead, changing demographics challenged the communities to think about how they could collectively create a public-private partnership to help newcomers assimilate into the community.

Chattanooga: A Real Joint Venture

In 1969, Chattanooga, Tennessee, received a "first" award for having the worst air quality in the nation. The air was filled with pollutants ranging from ozone to particulates to nitrous oxides emanating from the local munitions plant producing TNT. Chattanooga got itself in gear to respond. Working to accomplish more than the Environmental Protection Agency's recommended remedy, the city of Chattanooga and local groups set up a control board, initiated a public education campaign about pollution, and began to bring people together to talk about solutions. The effort worked, meeting air quality standards or exceeding them in five years (*Boundary Crossers*, 1997, p. 47).

The success of this process sent a message throughout the community: they could work together not just on pollution but on other issues. They set up a task force made up of people from across the community—elected officials, nonprofit leaders, business people, and interested citizens—to look at the community's future. Chattanooga had been hard hit not just by the recession but also by a changing economic base that had closed many local factories or made them obsolete. In the early eighties, the task force organized over sixty-five public meetings to sort through options. In the midst of the discussions, the task force visited Indianapolis, on the first of many "road trips" to get new ideas. That road trip produced a big idea: Chattanooga Venture. Indianapolis has had a twenty-five-year history of business leadership on critical civic issues. Formally called the Greater Indianapolis Progress Committee, this group used community-wide task forces to address and define economic and social issues in the city. Chattanooga Venture was Chattanooga's version of the progress committee. Incorporated in 1984, and funded for a decade by the local Lyndhurst Foundation, Chattanooga Venture had almost three thousand participants in its heyday (*Boundary Crossers*, 1997, pp. 41–42). The purpose was to bring Chattanoogans together to discuss and decide how the community would develop. Their motto was "to expedite positive community change through informed citizen involvement, to turn talk into action, to become the finest midsize city in America." Working on projects ranging from child care to historic preservation, the task forces began to look at every aspect of their shared community life.

The advent of Chattanooga Venture and related public-private partnerships caused former National Civic League president John Parr to dub it the "Chattanooga Process." According to Parr, citizens in Chattanooga have found a new way to work. They listen to all ideas; they work together to find answers; they have specific tasks but do not get locked in. The collective good is always the goal; preventing problems and creating positive change are the priorities; they always use the best talent and the best examples to generate local support and vision; and they learn from other communities. But they also had a vehicle to facilitate change: Venture. According to Rick Montague, formerly director of the Lyndhurst Foundation, "Every community needs a place where people with different agendas can come together to share ideas and work together" (*Boundary Crossers*, 1997, pp. 42, 54).

Chattanooga Venture's first effort, Vision 2000, established forty goals for the city. The initiative resulted in more than two hundred projects and programs, created almost fourteen hundred jobs, leveraged a financial investment of $793 million, and included seventeen hundred people. The results of Chattanooga's efforts at collaboration and partnership have been very impressive. By 1992, more than 90 percent of the goals had been completed or partially completed. The goals ranged from the development of the riverfront, to affordable housing, to advancement in human relations (*Boundary Crossers*, 1997, pp. 47–48). How did they do it?

These encompassing goals led to specific projects. For example, the Chattanooga Neighborhood Enterprise was established to take a creative financing approach to affordable housing issues. Human relations concerns led to the creation of the Human Rights/Human Relations Commission. The Tennessee Aquarium was built—the largest freshwater aquarium in the world. The people who participated in Vision 2000, as well as the people who watched, saw things happen.

The Chattanooga story makes partnership and collaboration look easy in hindsight. It wasn't. Getting people to come together around issues requires skill, commitment, and a local group as mediator, cheerleader, coordinator, and visionary. They had all this in Chattanooga Venture. They set goals and used them as a road map to determine what the community needed and how those needs could be met. They put a spotlight on success and let citizens, business, government, and nonprofits do the work. Was all smooth sailing? "There were naysayers," says Mai Bell Hurley, former Chattanooga Vision chairperson. "Some people were suspicious of the process but very few."

Chattanooga Venture itself has scaled down and moved shop to a local community college. Its initial work done, the organization is poised to act if called on but was not to be a self-perpetuating entity. The process itself is part of the fabric of the community. In 1999, discussions on urban sprawl brought out twenty-five hundred people. Chattanooga has figured out that a commonsense, inclusive approach to real problems allows the best to be attained from all citizens, encourages new ideas to be discussed, and creates a constituency for change. Chattanooga has shown that change will come from a comprehensive process that incorporates ideas from the community and is supported by decisive citizens working together to make change (Best Management Practices). Hurley says that the experience has changed the way Chattanooga does business forever. "Now almost any issue brings lots of people to community meetings. Now it's expected."

To visit Chattanooga today, the last thirty years would seem almost imaginary. There are still problems to be sure, but the physical appearance, population, and economic health are all quite different. Downtown has been rejuvenated; the waterfront has had a multimillion-dollar revitalization; many more projects are on the drawing board; but most important, the habit of working together is evident.

Communities create their map for change in different ways. Chattanooga learned from Indianapolis, Charlotte, and others, and many have learned from Chattanooga. Even with a tailored approach, there are some principles and practices that can ease the journey.

One of the smartest decisions that Chattanooga has made in the last twenty-five years was to create a structure that facilitated their ability to work together to address their *common* problems and opportunities. The next step for Chattanooga is to ensure that there is a process and a convenor in place that will be the catalyst for anticipating future issues. The thing we know for sure about community change is that it never ends. How did they know they were going in the right direction when Chattanooga Venture first started? Hurley said, "*I* didn't know, but *we* did."

Almena: An Idea for the Future

Communities sometimes see partnerships as the avenue of last resort and the *only* avenue out of their current situation. This was the situation in Almena, Wisconsin (population 720; U.S. Bureau of the

Census, 2000). The village of Almena, located in west central Wisconsin, is representative of the pressures facing rural areas nationwide and farming communities particularly. In the 1980s, the agricultural depression hit Almena hard, as did increasing competition from regional commercial and retail centers. The village lost its largest employer, Koser Silo, and with it several Main Street stores, including the only grocery store. Even though the community remained hopeful that things would turn around, there were few positive signs. Almena is a German settlement that reflects the values and attributes of its ancestors—toughness, stubbornness, and realism. This was a tough situation and they knew it.

Amid the downturn, the community decided to celebrate its centennial in 1987 with a weekend-long series of events. Citizens worked long hours to research local history, organize activities, and get the word out. The celebration brought out hundreds of people and produced two very important results: first, the successful organization and execution of the event showed the community that they could do something together; and second, they raised money. The Commercial Club (their chamber of commerce) decided to earmark $25,000 of the profits from the centennial to attract industry to Almena. They approached a regional community development organization, Impact Seven, for assistance. The strategic alliance with Impact Seven proved to be the catalyst and the guidance that the village needed. Impact Seven had been working in the region and the state since 1970. Its experience in encouraging economic development, job creation, and business expansion, particularly for low-income people, was just what Almena needed. Impact Seven has leveraged over $700 million for economic development in its history and has placed more than four thousand people in jobs. That track record was key for the village, and the interest in developing a comprehensive rural model was the incentive for Impact Seven. Their mutual interests brought the two together in a public-private partnership that included the Commercial Club, village administration, other local organizations, such as civic clubs, and later, Almena Business Development Corporation. The village groups joined together and pooled resources with one goal in mind—the revitalization of Almena. Rather than chase a myriad of singular projects, the group decided that all resources would be focused on the Almena Idea. The first step in the process was to identify the needs and priorities of the community. Over a three-day period of evening meetings, and through a questionnaire, citizens were able to articulate their visions to bring Almena back. The overall consensus was that the village had to have more commerce and industry in town. Their focus was to be on community redevelopment, which included jobs and revitalization of the community.

The Almena Idea included three key parts: marketing, infrastructure improvements, and financial assistance to firms interested in locating to Almena or expanding existing operations. To oversee these tasks, the Almena Business Development Corporation was created in 1990. Using state and federal loans and grants and *tax incremental financing,* the community created two industrial development parks (116 acres) to be used for business diversification and job creation. They began a marketing program to make the Almena business location opportunity known to business and industry. Their first bite was from an industrial development contract with the Farmers Home Administration in 1991 for the expansion of two businesses. That same year, the first new business arrived: L & M Gazebos, which added ten new jobs at peak production. Each subsequent year, more pieces began to fall into place. Money was raised for downtown revitalization, infrastructure improvements were made at the industrial park, and ground was broken on the Greater Wisconsin Business Center. In 1992, four additional businesses were added, and with them came twenty-five new jobs. In 1994 (just four years after the process began), the village established a Head Start program, with six new jobs, and added four other corporations, bringing thirty-five more jobs. In the last ten years, Almena has continued to grow, with the increase at 15 percent in a decade (Rural LISC Web site).

The Almena Idea goes far beyond jobs, however. The residents wanted their town back. A local bank razed a dilapidated building to create a new town square. A grant from the National Endowment for the Arts and matching local support allowed for the development of a downtown revitalization plan and the reawakening of Main Street. Further, the village planted trees, created small businesses, and even developed a trailhead for a local snowmobile–all-terrain-vehicle trail, called Cattail. The Almena Elementary School was not only saved, it was expanded. A facility for low-income seniors was opened. Impact Seven moved its offices to Almena. In total, the public-private partnership has attracted twenty-three new businesses or expansions, more than 142 jobs have been created, and 26 retained. The assessed tax base has increased by over $1.7 million on a total tax base of $7.34 million, primarily on new property.

The innovation of the Almena Idea, however, is due in part to the work of the "irritant," or organizer, in the turnaround. Almena needed that grain of sand that Impact Seven brought to the partnership to change the habits, attitudes, and practices that had become embedded in the community. In some situations, the loss of a major employer can galvanize a community to act. However, the cumulative losses are sometimes too much for a small community. A string of small-business losses coupled with the loss of a major employer creates a gloom-and-doom scenario. Failure becomes a self-fulfilling prophecy, fueled by cynicism, skepticism, and doubt. This is where the innovation of a strategic alliance is so necessary. In Almena's case, the alliance was composed of a community development corporation, Impact Seven; a local development corporation; and the village itself. Each party played a critical role in changing attitudes and creating one success at a time. Impact Seven brought a wealth of knowledge about rural economic development and community financing. The local development organizations provided capacity building within the existing community, which supported and furthered the project. The village itself devoted resources (time and money) to creating an environment where change could occur.

The role of the outside party, Impact Seven, cannot be underestimated in the process. It generated ideas and options that the village did not know existed. It not only brought management and organizational expertise to the table, which allowed the village to expand its reach for new business, but it also understood and explained the risks that accompany any new venture. The result? The outside irritant rocked the boat. It was a catalyst and a partner in creating new structures, and most important, it created an atmosphere of the "possible." Almena was not a quick fix. The parties involved brought a range of resources to bear around a strategy that would not only stabilize the community but give it new life and direction.

The replicability of the Almena Idea rests on these three elements: an outside irritant, local capacity, and the citizenry working together. It also rests on the ability of a community to supersede the turf battles and defensiveness of the past and be willing to clear the deck and organize for change. Almena's success can be measured by the long-term commitment of its citizens to keep the village healthy. It took time, risk, and constant encouragement to keep things moving. At times, it was difficult to remain hopeful, but citizens never gave up on their dream, no matter the risk or the criticism. What was the "Almena Idea" really? According to Mary Vinopal, housing developer and operations manager for Impact Seven, it was surely a public-private partnership that emphasized a unified economic development plan, but it was more. It was "getting the whole community together around revitalization—all the village worked together."

As the Almena story is analyzed and reanalyzed, one important fact is often lost. Almena was not just adding jobs—one by one or two by two—it was adding people, too. It rebuilt its community. The jobs were obviously a vehicle, but the real payoff is that there are now ninety-five more people living, working, and creating Almena's future.

Austin: The Wake-Up Call

Opportunities are born as well as problems solved when people can come together. Austin, Texas, was one of those cities that "woke up" to an opportunity, and that decision is paying dividends. In the early 1980s, Austin, Texas, was a stable state capital with a large university in its midst. Public sector institutions, including state, county, city, and the University of Texas, were the major employers. The stability of these organizations kept Austin's economy on an even keel. In the early sixties, branch plants of several major firms, like IBM, Texas Instruments, Lockheed, and Intel, brought good jobs to the area. IBM had a light manufacturing plant that produced Selectric typewriters and handheld calculators at its location. The Austin of the eighties was essentially a city of important pieces, but not a big picture. There were some real drawbacks in the way the city operated: some in the city were hostile to growth; the university was a presence, not a player; the nucleus of technology firms was small; and the mind-set was oil and gas (Henton, Melville, and Walesh, 1997, p. 43).

According to former mayor Kirk Watson, Austin's history can be tracked by three transitions. The first, he says, is the original design of the city. There are basically four dimensions: the river on one side, capitol hill on another, and creeks on the east and west. It was clear from even the early days that "capitol hill" and "college hill" would be prominent in the city's development. (The capitol dome and the tower of the University of Texas form a straight line.) The second transitional period came during the 1940s, says Watson, when the Colorado River was finally and successfully dammed. This brought increased electrical power to the area and allowed growth and development along the river's edge. During this period, however, there was an implied commitment that the business of Austin would be state government and higher education. There was not a concerted push for new industry.

The third transition began in 1983 and changed the economic landscape in Austin forever. With a light-manufacturing sector and a highly educated workforce in place, the community was ready to move to the next step. A strategy was developed by the chamber of commerce, the governor's office, the University of Texas, business people, citizens, and local leaders throughout the community to combat the declining economy and falling oil prices. The strategy focused on technology, and the goal was to land one of the biggest economic prizes of the decade—the Microelectronics Computer Technology Consortium. The winning community could look forward to significant research investment in laboratories and research facilities, an influx of scientists and technicians, and a big ticket to the prosperity of the twenty-first century. Austin found itself in competition with Research Triangle Park in North Carolina, San Diego, California, and other larger areas; in total, fifty-seven cities were in the competition. The working group of business people, college professors, progressive government leaders, and interested citizens met every morning for months to hone the strategy and to identify those elements of Austin that would make it more attractive than the competition. They emphasized the quality of the University of Texas, the public schools, cultural amenities, and quality of life—anything that would set Austin apart. This process and their successful application showed the community not only that leadership across sectors could work together but also that this effort could change the future of the region (Henton, Melville, and Walesh, 1997, p. 43). The presence and support of state government and the educational and research engine of the University of Texas were powerful vehicles for defining not only their technology thrust but also their future. This opportunity could go beyond Austin to help define a statewide economy.

In 1988, the city also won the SEMATECH competition and became home to a consortium of semiconductor manufacturers. That prize resulted in more development locally. The University of Texas developed a research park, and endowed thirty-two chairs in engineering and natural sciences (Henton, Melville, and Walesh, p. 43). Some would say that the base for Austin's success was built many years before when Defense Department moneys were invested there. It surely didn't hurt but many cities have had these kinds of investments and had not capitalized on them.

So where does modern-day Austin get its kick? Watson believes it was neither coincidence nor blind luck—the pieces were all in place. As he tells it, "It is not coincidence that Austin calls itself the 'live-music capital of the world.' The creativity that helped fuel the MCC and SEMATECH successes fuel the music industry." He gives example after example of the building blocks—such as large stores of intellectual capital; an emphasis on the environment and recreation; and the value of diversity of people, opinions, and ideas—that created the foundation that allowed Austin to fulfill its natural instincts of a creative economy. MCC and SEMATECH put Austin on the map in a technology sense, but Watson would argue that many mile markers were already in place.

There are many other places with state capitals and major universities that aren't doing nearly so well. In a series of articles for the *Austin-American Statesman,* two reporters began to search for some answers. First, they found that Austin has created an environment where people feel comfortable pushing the envelope. It is an open community that welcomes creative energy of all types, from technology to dance. Second, it is a community of ideas. Diversity of opinions is welcome. A third factor, they say, is Austin's openness to immigrants and newcomers. They bring with them expertise, a work ethic, and new ways of looking at the world. The authors quote William Frey who contends, "They [immigrants] revitalize the regions they move to and enrich them culturally with their tastes in music, food, and entertainment. The regions that do not attract [immigrants] have often experienced prolonged economic decline, or they lack the natural or cultural amenities that many migrants seek" (Lisheron and Bishop, 2002).

Fast-forward fifteen years, Austin has increased the number of patents it produces more than any other city in the United States. It submitted 74 patents to the U.S. Patent and Trademark office in 1975; in 2002, it submitted 2,014—a 27 percent increase (Bishop and Lisheron, 2002). Obviously, patents are only one barometer of economic growth, but they are illustrative of a shift of emphasis and investment. There are conflicting reasons for Austin's growth, of course. What is beginning to emerge as a primary factor harkens back to the eighties around those daily breakfast sessions.

Meeting the growing demand for a skilled workforce in the larger region has been a continuing challenge for Austin even with the downturn in the economy. Are there more challenges? Absolutely. Poverty and its related problems plague too many people in the community. The public schools are a continuing concern. However, Austin has the potential, the wherewithal, and the responsibility to lift all boats. It has done it before. Austin knows what it takes to create a "creative" community. Austin made smart decisions in the eighties. What has evolved is a culture of progress that invites, encourages, and supports working together in a creative, innovative, and open environment.

Fargo: Two Cities—One Community

One perception of partnerships is that they are created to "fix" things. However, it is often opportunities that offer organizations and agencies the chance to make real breakthroughs. It was an opportunity that created a partnership in Fargo, North Dakota, and neighboring Moorhead, Minnesota.

Why would a community in the upper reaches of the Midwest with a white population of more than 90 percent care about diversity? Lowell Wolff, community relations and planning director for the Fargo Public Schools, gave an answer. "We began to realize that with globalization, the biggest handicap we could hand our kids was an inability to work with other cultures" (Froslie, 2003). That sentiment and a commitment to include, rather than exclude, encouraged Fargo, North Dakota, to team with adjoining Moorhead, Minnesota, and two other neighboring communities to identify diversity as one of the top issues facing the region in 1993 and apply for outside funding from the Pew Partnership for Civic Change. Fargo (population 90,599) and Moorhead (population 32,177) are adjacent communities in two states, separated only by the Red River, but they see themselves as one community. Fargo was the eligible community selected for the grant, but they requested that Moorhead be listed with them.

In the early nineties, a group of community leaders drawn from the school system, social services, local government, and the non-profit community came together to address the mounting friction and assimilation issues of the area's growing population of migrant workers, primarily Hispanic, and the increased numbers of refugees who had been resettled in Fargo-Moorhead. Among the largest new ethnic groups were Bosnians, Sudanese, Kurds, and Somalis. This group of leaders believed, as a local editorial articulated, that "understanding the value of diversity is an education process. It comes easily to some, but not so easily to others" ("Ten Years of Doing Good Work," 2003). The team knew that they had to be proactive in creating a community where difference was not only accepted but also valued. With $100,000 from four local governments—Fargo and West Fargo in North Dakota and Moorhead and Dilworth in Minnesota—their two counties, Cass and Clay, the United Way, the community foundation, a local corporation, and a $400,000 grant from the Pew Partnership for Civic Change, Cultural Diversity Resources, Inc. was established in 1993.

During the decade that followed, the idea to embrace diversity took hold in the community with a range of services, outreach, and recognition. According to Yoke-Sim Gunaratne, executive director of Cultural Diversity Resources, Inc., "The larger community wanted to be proactive in addressing the diversity issue. The communities had had a long history of collaboration so it was natural to join together."

The staff and the board of the organization identified key areas where diversity issues emerged and where opportunities for service and education were clear: education, employment, housing, media, and health. Plans were developed in these areas by volunteer citizen action teams not only to educate but also to eliminate barriers that might exist on a broader agenda. One obvious barrier that crossed all issue areas was language. In 1997, the Community Interpreter Service was begun to schedule bilingual interpreters for more than forty-five hundred new residents who needed assistance navigating the community systems, according to Gunaratne. In one year, the client base for these services increased by 30 percent, with eleven languages offered. Cultural Diversity Resources became a source for local agencies for ways to better serve the new populations, as well as a resource to the newcomers themselves. In partnership with other agencies, they helped find housing, provided employment referrals, and assisted in medical interpretation through their Bridging the Gap program. In a particularly innovative partnership, Cultural Diversity Resources collaborated with the Clay County Public Health Department and the American Cancer Society to have bilingual outreach workers provide cancer education and prevention to the Hispanic, Native American, Vietnamese, and Kurdish communities, according to Gunaratne.

The description thus far sounds like a good program. It is certainly that. The uniqueness of this effort, however, is that the whole community made a smart decision over a decade ago to invest in a diversity strategy that has benefited all. When too many communities were wishing for the "good old days" when everybody looked alike, Fargo-Moorhead was changing with the times.

So what's changed in the last ten years? Almost five thousand people have learned about cultural differences through workplace and community training programs. The school system and parents have worked on an inclusive curriculum that embraces the many nationalities represented in the public schools. Mutual-assistance associations are forming in the Sudanese and Somali communities, and multiethnic leadership training has led to new people participating in community affairs. One of these new leaders, Sonia Hohnadel, one of the first volunteers to go through the multiethnic leadership program, was elected to the Moorhead School Board—the first Hispanic elected to serve. Elected officials were particularly supportive of the effort that lent legitimacy to the established communities and the newcomers, says Gunaratne. According to Fargo mayor, Bruce Furness, "They've [Cultural Diversity Resources] helped us avoid situations that some cities and communities have experienced. . . . They have helped the homogeneous community understand different cultures" (Froslie, 2003). The program met a need, but it also set the pace for the community to act and react in a different way. People have learned to value difference. Gunaratne says, "We are not seen as exotic or faddish but as playing a vital role in connecting the larger community to ethnic groups and vice versa."

Lessons Learned: In It Together for What?

These community illustrations examine very different issues, ranging from the environment to economic development to cultural diversity, but they all highlight key decisions by these communities to create a new direction. There are some commonalities, however, among the four. In each case, there is an outside "cause and effect" that prompted action. Chattanooga had economic and environmental challenges to address. Almena had an outside community development corporation that was both a partner and a catalyst. Austin had an incredible economic development opportunity. Fargo-Moorhead had a demographic change that presented challenges and opportunities. The point is that change is inevitable. If communities are organized to respond, adapt, and meet it head-on, they are way ahead of the game. If they can do it collectively, they are calling the game.

Organizing themselves for action took different tracks. In Chattanooga, the organizing process was led by community leaders and interested citizens. Clearly, the financial support of a local foundation was a key factor in the sustainability of the effort. Almena's organizing genius was the partnership with an outside agency to focus economic development efforts. In Austin, enlightened business, education, and government leaders, as well as interested citizens, made the vision that Austin could diversify its economic future around microelectronics a reality. Fargo-Moorhead's foundation of working together precedes the national emphasis on regionalism. Those communities have been working that way for decades. The Cultural Diversity Resources work was a natural link of their established relationships with nonprofits, the school systems, and local government.

Another less obvious theme runs through these examples and most others in the book. Communities have a sense of not only their own efficacy but also their own values. These communities had an idea of the kind of community they wanted and organized themselves to achieve it. This does not just happen on its own. It takes years of building trust, relationships, and a system of norms and expectations.

Getting Started in Your Community

Communities that want to change their patterns of work and relationships must begin with vehicles and projects to change the civic environment, but they also must identify those burning platform issues. Community organizers say that groups must build on small successes as they work toward fundamental change; the same is true at all levels of community work.

Working together can begin with small gatherings of people in a neighborhood who want to start a community garden or who are concerned about traffic; it can begin with joint projects between civic groups or religious organizations that have common concerns; or it can begin with a community-convening organization whose purpose is to bring people together on a range of common issues. Wherever you begin, be sure that the process is inclusive and definitive from the beginning. People will not make a commitment of time and energy to processes that exclude and have no specified purpose. The gatherings can be about a mutual concern, but they can also be about something fun—a street fair, a potluck, a book swap, or in my neighborhood, the annual Fourth of July parade of tricycles, baby carriages, and dogs. The important thing is focus.

As you think about improving the ability of your community to work together, look at patterns of interaction? Do the same people always turn up at the same meetings? Do you always talk to the same people? Are there places where people gather from across the community? Answering those questions will provide a better idea of the preliminary work that must be done to change the way your community does its joint work.

4

Building on Community Strengths

Everybody must realize the value they have. A community has a right to believe in itself; if it doesn't, no one else will believe in it either.

Becky Anderson

Any parent of a teenager can repeat the following litany verbatim: "There is nothing to do around here." Unfortunately, the dissatisfaction of young people with their communities is often shared by their parents. Many people really don't know their community. The problem, however, is not a recreational one. It is less about things to do and more about an understanding of a community's rich assets—human, physical, and organizational.

All too frequently, citizens and organizations who live and operate in a community, and the external agencies that do business there, see the silhouette of the community rather than the whole picture. Community impressions often do not go beneath the surface of problems and distress. For residents bombarded with the strains of everyday living, it is hard to separate the positives from the negatives. For outsiders, symptoms of decline suggest more to come. Distressed communities are painted with a broad brush of deficits without any real regard for what or who has gifts to give. Communities have "half-full–half-empty" complexes, just like individuals.

Framing the Issues

The goal of this chapter, first and foremost, is to convey an idea. Community work that turns on the assets of a community rather than on its deficits has a better chance of successfully addressing problems. Leading with strengths has been the mantra of successful communities and successful people for years. Some would say that it is just an attitude. I would say that it is much more.

The residents of 138th Street in Harlem probably passed the Abyssinian Baptist Church every day. Little did they know that the congregation was the asset they needed to begin to rebuild their neighborhood and their livelihood. The men and women in western North Carolina came to understand how the long-held craft tradition throughout their region could be the impetus for a new approach to economic and community development that protected the environment and provided living-wage incomes. The commercial development districts in twenty-two neighborhoods in Boston are a new link to making neighborhood shopping viable and desirable again. Building on the wealth of assets within neighborhoods, the Boston Main Streets program is working with them to be destinations, not passbys. Fremont's experience has shown that building neighborhood structures using the assets approach creates a foundation for relationships and common action that is durable and sustainable.

The illustrations you will read are not about the optimists versus the pessimists; they are about the realists versus the idealists. People who know communities and have studied them know well the virtues of leading and creating from the gifts, talents, and resources that people have rather than from what they don't have. We are learning that this approach is the only sustainable change strategy. The asset strategy does not gloss over deficits—there are still systemic problems to solve—but it does create processes and systems so that people see themselves and their communities differently. It helps people know that they are part of the solution, not part of the problem.

What Happened to Communities?

For decades, the nation has tried to "fix" the effects of disinvestment, racial tension, and suburbanization, which have taken their toll on cities. Likewise rural areas have suffered from job loss, the lack of a high-tech economy, few investments, and chronic poverty. In both instances, outside resources have been brought into the communities to stem the decline.

Since the sixties, hundreds of programs have been initiated. Neighborhood revitalization efforts have been marked by invention, and then later reinvention, of neighborhood institutions. These organizations were activated and reactivated, especially during times of social and racial attention and concern for cities and their citizens (Halpern, 1995, p. 2). It became clear, however, that there were issues facing many communities, such as generational poverty, widely available illegal drugs, and increased crime and violence, which were not going away on their own. In response, the nation initiated the Great Society program and such initiatives as the Model Cities program, Urban Development Action Grants, and VISTA. These interventions, and the later enterprise and empowerment zones, were designed to improve some of the country's poorest communities with a combination of community renewal, jobs programs, technical assistance, and any other intervention that might work.

The approaches and kinds of interventions have been driven in part by the changes in the communities themselves. We have already discussed the dramatic ethnic and demographic change in some places. There have also been shifts in investment of those outside the community, a significant change in the economic climate, and a change in patterns of settlement (Halpern, 1995, p. 3). The Annie E. Casey Foundation described life in too many urban communities: "Almost 20 percent of households do not have a telephone at home and 50 percent do not have a car" (2002, p. 9). This condition has contributed to the economic and social fragility of the urban neighborhood. In the case of rural America, communities have lost thousands of well-paying low-skill jobs, particularly in textiles and low-tech manufacturing. Of the 200 persistently poor counties (those with at least a 20 percent poverty rate), 195 of them are rural (U.S. Bureau of the Census, 1997). Connections to technology, transportation, living-wage jobs, and access to social services are extremely limited in the poorest rural areas. The "have" and "have-not" communities are pretty easy to identify no matter where they are located.

Although the last forty years have seen aspects of community improvement, the cost-benefit ratio of community investment to positive results is relatively low. There have been clear signs of success in some places, but overall our national interventions have failed to achieve the change hoped for or expected. Some would argue that the nation as a whole wrote off poor, distressed communities as hopeless and beyond help. With that resignation, they argue, came the inability or the unwillingness to stay the course and get at the root of the problems. Instead, as Kenneth Clark observed about the similarity of recommendations on some of America's most destructive riots—Watts (1972), Chicago (1919), and Harlem (1935 and 1943)—"It's a kind of Alice in Wonderland with the same moving picture re-shown over and over again, the same analysis, the same recommendations and the same inaction" (Kerner Commission, 1968, p. 265, cited in Halpern, 1995, p. 16).

For too many people, daily life is consumed by mere survival, and opportunities for a better future appear inaccessible (Committee for Economic Development [CED], 1995). Too many efforts to fix problems have missed the mark. In a nation that has excelled at technology developments, it's puzzling why more progress has not been made in eliminating the systemic problems in our society or at least reducing them significantly? One reason is a general perception by many Americans about why the poor are poor and why "bad" neighborhoods are "bad." Halpern (1995, p. 6) argues that despite evidence to the contrary, Americans think of poverty, for example, as an individual, locally placed problem that is a product of individual shortcomings and unhealthy community conditions.

The external factors, such as the availability of living-wage jobs; changing labor market; demand for new skills; and racial, economic, and social exclusion, do not seem to figure into the equation. For many people, "The poor could do better if they wanted to." This perception puts people and their problems into boxes. Separated from the reality from which they live and survive, poor people "are presented as mere aggregations of personal cases, each with its own logic and self-contained causes" (Wacquant and Wilson, 1989, p. 9). This is not to say that people in distressed communities don't make their share of unwise decisions. They certainly do. However, the primary difference between poor people and others is the tremendous impact of life choices and mistakes when there is so little room for error (Halpern, p. 6). Too often, we have organized our "help" for distressed communities with these misconceptions in mind.

Turning the Tide

On streets, in neighborhoods, and in whole towns across America, there are signs of hope and reinvigoration. In some places, the downward spiral has not just stopped; it has reversed. There are isolated reasons in some places—new industry, a revitalized area, new leadership—but the overall improvement can usually be attributed to building the capacity of people in a neighborhood, community, or city to act for themselves. People have discovered that there is "plenty to do around here" and plenty of people who can get it done.

Why Some Communities Fare Better Than Others

Years of observation and research at the Pew Partnership has found that successful communities are those that foster positive relationships with their residents. These communities have places where information is exchanged and citizens interact; they encourage residents to identify and work toward common goals; and they solicit resources and partners outside their boundaries. These communities are not isolated from their problems or their solutions. They are building and sustaining their avenues of social capital while improving their human, civic, and physical capital (Committee for Economic Development, 1995, p. 3). Despite the obvious barriers and obstacles, these communities are moving forward not backwards.

There are numerous opinions on why some distressed communities do better than others, even those with comparable negative and positive characteristics. Some say that it is a key intervention at the right time, a problem not allowed to get out of hand. Another group believes that it is the stability of residency and home ownership. Still others say that it is the social fabric of the neighborhood that has allowed citizens to have some control over their lives and build relationships. In Robert Putnam's research for *Bowling Alone* (2000), a study of social networks in communities across the country, he found that communities, even poor ones, with some level of social capital tend to have lower crime rates and better relationships. Robert Sampson's research shows that some communities are safer than others because of the fabric of the community and residential stability. Studies controlled for poverty and other negative community factors show that crime hits communities hardest where teenagers are left unsupervised, where there are sparse relationships or anonymity among residents, and where there is low participation or few connections in local activities (Sampson, 1999).

Solutions for Rebuilding Communities

Communities will be rebuilt and empowered when effective public policies are joined with renewed efforts to strengthen all capital investments within communities. Neither is a substitute for the other (Committee for Economic Development, 1995). Efforts to build capital of all types require that there be permanent, sustainable organizations in communities, which serve as anchors for overall development efforts. More and more foundations, governments, nonprofits, and businesses have realized the power of effective community-based organizations that believe that people—all people—bring assets to the community table that are valuable and critical to overall community success. They just need to be tapped.

The notion of community building has evolved from a clear set of experiences and research that point to the fact that community revitalization comes from a combination of factors. Angela Glover Blackwell, president and CEO of PolicyLink in Oakland, California, defines community building as "continuous, self-renewing efforts by residents, community leaders and professionals engaged in collective action aimed at problem-solving and enrichment that result in improved lives and greater equity and produce new or strengthened institutions, organizations, relationships, and new standards and expectations for life in the community" (Blackwell, National Community Building Network). This encompassing definition highlights the inclusiveness of the process, the elements of action and expectations, but most important, the continuity of community building. It is not a seminar or technical-assistance workshop. Community building is about the actions and activities that happen every day. It cannot rise and fall with one program or one grant.

Community building efforts are under way through a number of organizations both inside and outside the communities. While applying a particular set of strategies, each has the general mission of getting the community on its feet again, with residents having a full set of tools and skills at their disposal. These organizations fall under several well-known rubrics: community development corporations, comprehensive community initiatives, community-based organizations, neighborhood associations and settlement houses, local development corporations, and national intermediaries (Chaskin, Brown, Venkatesh, and Vidal, 2001, pp. 15–22). These organizations leverage money; provide technical assistance; provide links to social services; offer services themselves, such as child care and job training; and act as switching stations for a broad range of economic and community development activities. In addition, religious organizations and other local organizations have extended their mission and their reach to include community development. These organizations and institutions have broadened the capacity of communities to take control of their own futures. Giving people a realistic sense that change can happen and results can be different creates a mental and tangible reality. People who do not know anyone with a job can begin to imagine what working might be like. Children who never thought about college are thinking about it—for themselves. The bar is set so that it can be jumped. The conversation shifts from what we don't have to what we do have, from what we can't get to what we can get, and from what the community is to what the community should be.

Sustainable community building happens when the public is engaged, not just persuaded, and when the community has a sense of what it has in itself—its inner strengths. In many low-income communities, what is most visible is what's missing (grocery stores, neighborhood retail stores, and well-kept homes and apartments) and the bad things that are there (too many unemployed people on street corners, too many abandoned buildings and cars, and too much glass on the playgrounds). Amid those two stark scenarios are people, organizations, and institutions that could affect the situation and provide the missing piece of the solution.

Community Building: More Than Buildings

Community building undergirds the creation of social capital and provides a foundation from which a community can grow and build. It is a state of mind as well as a development strategy that allows a person or a group of people to be energized by possibility, not defeated by inadequacy. This is not to imply that financial or technical assistance is not needed; quite the contrary is true. But that assistance—internal or external to the community—can be complementary to existing resources and capacities that have been long overlooked. As the CED report concludes, "Community building alone will not revitalize communities, but no initiative will succeed without it" (Committee for Economic Development, 1995, p. 2).

Developing a Community from Within

Creating a community's ability to change its own future can take several approaches. It can focus largely on organizations and individuals; it can focus on effective connections and shared values; and it can focus on civic participation and engagement. There *is* agreement about the fundamentals that must be in place for capacity building to take place: existence of resources broadly defined, networks of relationships, strong leadership, and vehicles for collective action and problem solving. However, there is not consensus on how the factors interact or their impact (Chaskin, Brown, Venkatesh, and Vidal, 2001, pp. 7, 11).

In order to realize our assets, we must know who and what are in a community and leverage their collective gifts, talents, and resources for the good of the whole community. The ability to champion our strengths while working diligently on our deficits builds a community's capacity to act on its own behalf. This capacity makes communities work by bringing together human capital, organizational resources, social capital, and outside assistance to galvanize citizens to take responsibility and leverage all their collective resources to improve their community (Chaskin, Brown, Venkatesh, and Vidal, 2001, p. 7).

Another critical step in the ability of a community to steer its future is to name the problem it is trying to solve. All too often, the fix-it mentality takes over and symptoms get all the attention. Every community builder would agree that tangible results help fuel revitalization efforts, but they can also derail them. If community residents are not a part of naming and framing the real problems, then the road taken may not get to the desired destination. For example, reducing gang violence may be a *subgoal* to the larger goal of getting young people in legitimate jobs and teaching them skills. Obviously, the strategy for change would be very different depending on the primary goal. Years of valuable community research from the Kettering Foundation (1998, pp. 16–18) has found that unless a community issue is understood from multiple perspectives and takes into account different interests, it is unlikely that citizens can work together as a community.

Place or People, Process or Outcome

The discussion of community building falls under a general category of *community development*. This is the process that creates local organizations to help identify, build, and expand the assets of the community (Green and Haines, 2002, p. 8). Historically, planners, community development specialists, and urban policy specialists have debated whether community development is about *place or people* or about *process or outcome*. Place-based development has guided the community development movement for almost forty years. The thesis of this argument is that considerable investments must be made in improving "place" before people can benefit. In community development corporations (CDCs), for example, housing has been a predominant focus of the movement for many years. Now the CDC movement and other community-based organizations have moved to a more comprehensive, holistic approach to strengthening distressed areas. The belief is that investing in people as a primary goal may misfire if you prepare them for jobs that can't be found in the area (Green and Haines, 2002, p. 7). However, Halpern (1995, p. 11) cautions that it is always a struggle to address both the structure of opportunities, such as jobs, and the individual's ability to realize the opportunity.

Communities, no matter their location, must have an infrastructure of affordable housing, job access, and business development, but simultaneously there must be an emphasis on improving the chances of individuals to succeed through their own efforts. Part of the problem with choosing place over people is that there is an expectation that if place were improved, then community organizations could solve local problems such as unemployment or housing, address inequities around wealth and power, encourage democratic values and citizenship, improve the prospect for individuals, and create a sense of community without significant investments in people. This is a powerful agenda to be locked into a place-or-people investment strategy (Rubin and Rubin, 1992).

In reality, however, community change involves place *and* people. In a 1967 speech to the Senate, Senator Robert F. Kennedy said that we needed to support the migration of the poor out of the ghetto, but at the same time we cannot forget the place or the people left behind. There are those, he said, "who would build their own community, take pride in their own neighborhoods, if they could" (Peirce, 1993).

The process-or-product debate is a little fuzzier to track and also to understand. Certain processes empower people in a community to act on behalf of their own common interests. Those processes are often community organizing, leadership development, and coalition building. At the same time, the sustainability of those processes is driven by results. Both are necessary and critical to community capacity building. For the person who asks, "Should we build affordable housing or start a job-training program or organize a youth leadership program in our community," the answer is *yes*.

Community development is about people, place, process, and outcomes. The needle cannot be moved permanently until attention is paid to building the capacity of the community to work together (people and process) to create results where people live (place and outcome). Scattering our approach or favoring one angle over the other can minimize the long-term effect. It is not an either-or argument. "It matters less what is built than that the projects introduce assets, both material and social, for those in neighborhoods of deprivation. These assets create an economic stake in society, for both recipients and the community-based development organization, as well as a set of obligations—paying rent, maintaining property, concern with the quality of the neighborhood—that is socially empowering" (Rubin, 2000, p. 162).

Asset-based development is common sense. Empowering people to realize the resources and ideas they have to offer is a critical first step for personal self-sufficiency. The inspiring stories that we read from poor neighborhoods or public housing are natural phenomena that occur when people take charge of their lives and their neighborhoods.

Finding the Assets in a Community

Though the search for the best method of community building continues, three organizations—*community development corporations, local development organizations,* and *neighborhood organizations*—are proven vehicles for building the capacity for low-income communities to change their odds for success. They most often focus on people and place and on process and product, and they address both the tangible and intangible dimensions of community building. Their experiences give pointers on ways that communities can reposition themselves for success, not failure. Community development cousins, each works from a theory of change that more can be accomplished when residents have a role and a stake in the outcome. Although they are different in their missions and approaches, all three are rooted in the notion that communities have considerable capacity to change, that citizens in those communities have valuable untapped assets, and that investments must be made to develop all forms of capital. Every person in the country ought to understand how these ideas can change the way communities do their work.

Research by two Northwestern University professors, John McKnight and John Kretzmann, provided direction on how asset identification can change how work is done in a community. Observations from their work with low-income communities over many years has added definition and process to the asset dimension of community development. In their work on Chicago's East Side, they found poverty and distress for sure, but they also found more than three hundred voluntary associations and neighborhood groups, many of which were unknown or untapped by the "helpers" who had come to work in the community. As they continued their study of low-income communities, they found volunteer organizations, communities of faith, established businesses, institutions, and other community organizations in *all* low-income communities. These community resources brought "assets" to the community renewal efforts. Kretzmann and McKnight (1993) contend that there are two general approaches to community development, and the approach that is taken can make all the difference. The first, they write, "begins by focusing on a community's needs, deficiencies and problems, is still the most traveled, and commands the vast majority of our financial and human resources. The alternative route . . . begins with a clear commitment to discovering a community's capacities and assets" (p. 1).

Deficit-Driven Approach to Community Development

The deficit-driven approach starts with a delineation of all the problems that exist in a community—unemployment, slum housing, and crime, for example—and helps citizens understand how services from the outside can meet their needs and affect their problems. In Kretzmann and McKnight's words, "As a result, many low-income urban neighborhoods are now environments of service where behaviors are affected because residents come to believe that their well-being depends on being a client. They begin to see themselves as people with special needs that can only be met by outsiders" (1993, p. 2).

It is easy for citizens to fall into this web of deficiency and dependency because many funding sources, research projects, and the media focus on what is wrong, not what is right. However, Kretzmann and McKnight argue that building on assets is not as much altruistic as it is a commonsense approach. They identify two realities in the needs-based approach: first, the research and evidence show that successful community development takes place when local people are involved and invest their time, energy, and resources in making change. Second, there are fewer and fewer resources available for large-scale outside interventions. "The hard truth, they write, is that development must start from within the community, and in most of our urban neighborhoods, there is no other choice" (p. 5).

Asset-Driven Approach to Community Development

Focusing on assets when the statistics are overwhelmingly negative and the long-term outlook bleak creates new possibilities for residents and the community organizations that work with them. The assets and capacities that already exist in communities must be the foundation for community development. The key to neighborhood regeneration "is to locate all the available assets in the local community, to begin connecting them with one another in ways that multiply their power and effectiveness, and to begin to harness local institutions that are not yet available for local development purposes" (Kretzmann and McKnight, pp. 5–6).

Identifying community assets begins by challenging people to think about their own lives differently. Every person has gifts, skills, and capacities that communities need. Young people, seniors, welfare mothers, the physically challenged, and you and I have things to bring to the table that we have never even thought about. Shifting the focus to assets not deficits is not a low-income strategy; it is one that can benefit every community and all of our lives. Kretzmann and McKnight have developed very thorough surveys that communities can use to gather asset information about individuals, citizen associations, and local institutions. Although it is time intensive to build a *community inventory*, it is essential to the understanding of how and where the community might develop itself. There are two guiding premises, however, that should be noted. An *asset map* is not an academic exercise to develop bar charts for benchmarking or statistical tables. It is an interactive way to connect individuals to their own talents and empower them to use them; it is a way to collect the depth and breadth of already-existing organizations and the resources and activities they offer. Second, asset-mapping is an opportunity to name the institutions that are permanently located in the community and establish contact and relationships. In a nutshell, asset mapping allows a community to know itself and imagine a different set of relationships and interactions on its own behalf. In other words, it is not just a map.

The asset-mapping process requires different data-gathering techniques depending on whether the assets are found in individuals, citizen associations, or local institutions (Kretzmann and McKnight, 1993, pp. 14–18). To map individual capacities, citizens are asked to verbally respond to a series of questions or in some cases complete the questionnaire themselves. The questions center on four main areas:

1. *Skill information*, the first section, asks about the skills people have learned at home, in the community, or at the workplace.
2. *Community skills*, the second section, asks what kind of work people have done in the community and what kind they would be willing to do.
3. *Enterprising interests*, the third section, asks about where people have considered starting a business or if they are presently involved in a business.
4. *Priority skills*, the last section, deals with personal information, asking citizens to say what they are best at doing.

In order to create an asset map of local associations and organizations, Kretzmann and McKnight (pp. 109–119) suggest newspapers, directories, and other printed sources; word of mouth or suggestions from citizens; and telephone surveys. What does the local association map provide? It essentially gives an inventory of all the many organizations, from study clubs to political organizations to artistic groups. There are many informal groups in every community, so it requires digging deep to find all of them. What this map does not tell you is what the organizations really do and what programs they offer. This can provide a mother lode of extremely valuable information for building community resources and making connections among and between groups and individuals.

For those people who say, "There is nothing here in my community," a listing of organizations that are permanently placed in a community, like schools, banks, hospitals, churches, synagogues, and mosques; police stations; and federal offices, will produce a long list. However, Kretzmann and McKnight found that the presence of these organizations in a community does not necessarily translate to community connectedness. In fact, some of these organizations see their location as only a place to work and have no involvement or interest in the surrounding community.

Originally used in large urban areas, the asset-mapping process is equally useful in small cities and rural communities. The fundamental payoff of this approach comes when people see that they and their neighbors are capable of taking charge of their lives and the future of their community. Having all this information about assets is no guarantee, however, that things are going to get better. It needs a delivery system. That system can be rooted in the many community-based organizations that operate from the asset model of change. There are community development corporations, local community development organizations, and neighborhood associations and groups that understand what it means to build from assets not deficits. These organizations have seen the hopelessness that occurs when a community and its residents think and act as if they have nothing to offer, only services to receive. As one of the most famous college basketball coaches of our time, Duke's Coach Mike Krzyzewski, once said, "Teams have to own their own team" to be successful. The same can be said for communities. They must be the owners and the authors of their future. The four examples discussed in this chapter approach asset building from different perspectives. They are using the contacts, resources, and partnerships inside the community to strengthen the ability of people in the community to do their own work together and to connect to those outside the community in a different way. The commitment to having poor neighborhoods define their needs and assets, have a strong say in their own fate, and work toward making communities not only viable but sustainable is the key to community change that we seek (Halpern, 1995, p. 127).

Four very different venues and experiences have been selected for identifying and building on community assets. These four approaches to asset-based development and community building turn on that idea—there is lots to build on. Each represents a particular type of community building organization. The Abyssinian Development Corporation is a community development corporation that grew out of the concerns of a large African American church whose neighborhood was suffering the ravages of neglect, disinvestment, and deficit mentality. HandMade in America is a local development organization that works in rural America, where needs are great but so are heart and hand. (Their story also extends to the Small Towns Revitalization Project, an offshoot of Hand-Made in America.) Boston Main Streets is a citywide, government-sponsored, community-based organization whose mission is to improve local commercial districts and revitalize the social and economic prospects of neighborhoods. Fremont, California, demonstrates a new approach by local government to neighborhood development built on relationships, connections, and assets.

Community Development Corporations

Community development corporations have as primary goals to serve low-income communities and to empower residents (National Congress for Community Economic Development, 1999). CDCs vary in size, but all of their work is toward the revival and development of distressed and low-income communities. Affordable housing is probably the issue for which they are best known. In the early days, it was thought that housing was a way for residents to get invested in the process (Halpern, 1995, p. 141). The reach of CDCs goes far beyond housing today. They encourage financial investment in communities; they improve or create commercial and industrial space; they make loans to small business; and they offer job-training programs, child care, and even supermarkets. CDCs and community development financial institutions (CDFIs) have also been instrumental in developing community loan funds that make money available to low-income people to start a business, buy a house, and so forth. For example, one of the most successful of those organizations is the Center for Community Self-Help in North Carolina, which has leveraged more than $1.78 billion in financing for almost twenty-six thousand home buyers, small businesses, and nonprofits to create ownership and economic opportunities for minorities, women, rural residents, and low-wealth families (Center for Community Self-Help Web site).

Most CDCs were created because residents finally said to themselves and one another that something had to be done inside the community to improve things—the supposed tried and true ways of help from the outside were not working. The improvement they sought was not another temporary or stop-gap approach to the real issues of generational poverty and disinvestment but a real path out. As Paul Grogan and Tony Proscio write in *Comeback Cities* (2000), "'Changing things' means seeking investment, developing or renovating property, building on assets, and generally drawing power and capital into the community, rather than scare it away" (p. 67). This sense of building the communities from within was to take on a life of its own. The CDC is a lever for people who lived in the neighborhood to change their economic futures, using market forces and public-private investment. "They are to urban development," according to Grogan and Proscio, "what start-up companies and new technologies are to the business world: a channel through which individual energies and ingenuity tap and transform the broader market" (p. 69).

Overall CDCs have developed seventy million square feet of commercial and community facilities, supported almost six thousand businesses, built or rehabbed thousands of homes, and initiated a multitude of neighborhood programs. Communities that have been most successful with their CDCs understand that they have assets to build on, that there is hope, and that partnerships must be built (National Congress for Community Economic Development, 1999).

The CDC movement has put both power and resources in the hands of communities that can be used *by* the community *for* the community. A critical step in the CDC process is for community residents to see themselves and their neighbors as problem solvers not just problems. There is considerable capacity building linked to CDC organizations through technical assistance, but it is a mindset that must be cultivated if communities are to move forward.

Abyssinian Development Corporation: A Church with a Mission

Harlem is almost a city within a city. With a rich artistic and cultural tradition, this part of upper Manhattan has been home to some of the great artists of our time, such as Langston Hughes, Zora Neale Hurston, Countee Cullen, and Jean Toomer. Yet among this cultural imprint has been a gradually declining infrastructure and social system. Disinvestment by building owners, the city, and local residents, coupled with growing unemployment in the sixties and seventies and racial unrest, resulted in a distressed community with incredible needs juxtaposed against incredible assets.

One of the things that remained constant in Harlem over time was the presence of religious organizations. None was so well known as the Abyssinian Baptist Church on 138th Street. Founded in 1808 by free blacks and named after Ethiopian (Abyssinian) seamen, the church had always had a strong outreach in the community. In 1986, the church leaders and members began to think about how to affect the community's long-term future. As they organized ad hoc planning and implementation groups within the congregation, they began to see the need for a more comprehensive approach. It was not just a question of substandard housing but also a lack of child care, lack of jobs, lack of access to services; the neighborhood needed this and more to move forward. The parishioners knew that producing housing without the various family supports needed to keep people in housing was not the way to go. Their broad goal, wherever it took them, was to improve, assist, and revitalize the neighborhood surrounding the church with the full participation of the community. Their target area was the central Harlem community between 125th and 139th Streets and between Fifth and St. Nicholas Avenues, approximately.

Years of disinvestment had left Harlem in disrepair and in despair. Nowhere was it as obvious as on West 138th Street. As one person described it, "The street and surrounding streets looked like hell." Directly across the street from the church were boarded-up buildings and a vacant lot. The lot had been equipped for a playground, but vandalism and shifting soil had left most of the equipment upside down. The neighborhood was primarily African American, many unemployed and on welfare, and most living in substandard housing or no housing at all. The city of New York owned a majority of the property in the area by virtue of private absentee owners walking away: the city became the landlord of necessity if the buildings were left standing. The late Reverend Samuel Proctor, then pastor of Abyssinian, and a group of parishioners vowed that something had to be done to stop the bleeding in the neighborhood—literally and figuratively.

With this goal and a $50,000 seed grant from the Local Initiatives Support Corporation in hand, the church made a decision to establish the Abyssinian Development Corporation (ADC) in 1989. Then senior pastor Calvin Butts III hired one of the church's own to run it. Karen Phillips, an experienced community-planning, real estate development, and urban-design professional, and others went to work—and work they did. Their first task was to meet with their neighbors face-to-face and explain their goals. Although the church was a formidable presence in the neighborhood, says Phillips, "We wanted to be sure that we didn't force the development down people's throats. The clear message from the beginning was that 'we are your neighbors, we want to work with you.' Our slogan was 'we don't want to do things to people or for them.'"

The new organization quickly determined the assets that they had at their disposal. First, there was the church itself. The faith and outreach of the congregants were a huge part of the project and its process. According to Phillips, that presence cannot be under-estimated. Second, there was the gold mine of housing stock that remained, which was beautifully detailed and well built. Even years of neglect had not eroded its potential. And third, there were the people themselves. The first step in the acquaintance process was to reactivate the twenty-two block associations. Led by local leaders, these block associations began the process of reconnecting neighbor to neighbor and were also a valuable conduit for information and neighborhood feedback.

The corporation began with a very visible project—homeless housing directly across the street from the church. This project showed movement with support of the congregation, but it also raised the ire of some on the local community board, who objected to what they called "defacing the church" with a shelter across the street. The corporation went on to rehabilitate housing, start a four-hundred-child Head Start program, create the Thurgood Marshall Academy for Learning and Social Change, and establish a public intermediate and high school that emphasizes leadership development. In one of its most visible projects, ADC negotiated and opened the first supermarket in Harlem in decades, the Pathmark Store. Did everyone agree with the directions taken? Certainly not. There was concern from small grocers about the impact of the supermarket. They were afraid that Pathmark would put them out of business. Instead, says Phillips, the ADC helped the small grocery owners become more competitive by helping them get better terms for financing their capital improvements. The stores improved their stock and their services, and more customers shopped in the community. There were naysayers and doubters, who objected to other pieces. Today, however, 138th Street and surrounding streets and avenues are visibly different. There are still a few vacant buildings around and people's circumstances are still not great, but there is a feeling of hope and possibility.

Why has this effort worked when so many have failed? According to Karen Phillips, currently a senior consultant with CAMIROS and a member of the New York City Planning Commission, there

were three elements that made the difference: first, having the support of the church leadership. They trusted the design and the program management and supported and believed in the vision for
change. Second, the project had the credibility of the church combined with the faith and political sophistication of the members.
Since 1808, Abyssinian Baptist Church had ministered to the needs
of people of African American descent; the corporation and its outreach was another evolution of that work. The church sent a strong
message to the community that they were not only a credible partner but also in the neighborhood to stay. This was key to neighborhood buy-in. The third factor pertained to the political ties,
partnerships, and connections of the church leadership. At a time
when too many poor communities were written off by the political
establishment, the Reverend Calvin Butts III was a powerful force
in making financial and political connections outside the community and keeping people engaged in the work. However, there is a
fourth factor not on Phillips's list: her own leadership and other
leaders before and after her, such as Dr. Butts, Dr. Proctor, Darian
Walker, and many unnamed community resources. Their vision saw
the original investment of $50,000 soar to over $200 million
invested in the community from diversified funding sources.

There is plenty left to do, but change has happened in central
Harlem. In addition to scores of rehabilitated housing for families
and seniors, nearly four hundred thousand square feet of commercial space has been created. Small's Paradise Jazz Club, once a popular stop and landmark in Harlem, is now set aside for commercial
use and as a new home for the Thurgood Marshall Academy. Jobs
have been created at Pathmark and elsewhere. Families are being
better served through social programs.

Lessons Learned: Start Where You Are

The key to the success of the Abyssinian Development Corporation was an asset that has been in Harlem since 1923 and in New
York City for almost two centuries: a church. According to Phillips,
the human and political assets of this church and others in

predominantly African American communities can be the turnkey for change. She believes that they are the only remaining vehicle that the community can own and control itself. It is a place for educating poor people who are outside the economic system on ways to get control of their own lives. The institutional and religious strength of a church paved the way for the work of the Abyssinian Development Corporation. I suspect they might say that God provided the map.

Local Development Corporations

Local development corporations have been around in different forms for decades, as both nonprofit and for-profit organizations. Local development organizations work in a range of areas, from industrial recruiting to developing industrial parks to historic preservation to working in neighborhoods. They provide low-cost loans to start-up businesses, establish business incubators, and develop public-private partnerships. They help communities think about their future in new ways. Sometimes this manifests itself in a visioning process. Typically, communities begin by asking themselves three questions: What do people want to *preserve* in this community? What do people want to *create* in this community? And what do people want to *change* in this community? Answers to these questions help groups focus on the big issues. These kinds of "big-picture" processes translate into doable projects and initiatives that lead to bigger goals. Citizens in communities come to understand the uniqueness of their community and know that one model doesn't fit all. If participation in economic development is inclusive and comes from all parts of the community, the process and the leadership are impartial, there is attention to detail, risks are taken, short-range and long-range goals are set, and media are interested, then results will occur (Klein, Benson, Anderson, and Herr, 1993, pp. 10–19).

Communities have been lulled into the deception of not recognizing either their strengths or their weaknesses. Local development organizations help provide a realistic appraisal of their situation and alternative directions. Grogan and Proscio (2000), p. 69) write very persuasively that the spark for real community development comes when people in the neighborhood get really fed up: a "we are not gonna take it anymore" kind of attitude. This approach makes sense to all of us: people finally rallying for themselves, not looking for the hand *out* but the hand *up*. In the case of western North Carolina, it started with the hand *made*.

Handmade in America: Crafting Community Development

Western North Carolina is a model of the glass half full. Nowhere has the application of asset-based, citizen-led community development been better exercised. Located in the Appalachian range of North Carolina, the twenty-two counties of western North Carolina have historically been the poor relation to the more prosperous Piedmont and eastern sections of the state. Graced with incredible natural beauty, the region's economic development initiatives have always had to consider the presence of mountains and uneven terrain in their pursuits. Citizens value the pristine nature of their surroundings and want to keep it that way. When other areas were courting automobile plants and chasing smokestacks, western North Carolina was never in the running. Part of the economic development challenge is its mountainous terrain and the availability of land generally. The U.S. Forest Service and the National Park Service account for 55 to 60 percent of land control (HandMade in America, 1995).

Economic development in rural areas often presents different challenges and opportunities because of geographical isolation, lack of technology, sparse populations, and a limited number of trained workers. Efforts to attract economic development to rural areas have tended to follow two paths: (1) the development of industrial parks and the offering of tax abatements and (2) microenterprise and small-business incubator programs. In the mountains of western North Carolina, neither one of these "fixes" seemed appropriate. A mountainous terrain does not have the kind of flat land that large industrial complexes need, and further, rural communities are often resistant to large takeovers by outsiders of their land, their economy, and some might say their lives. The best approach to rural economic development is *community* economic development. Rural economies need a rigorous strategic analysis to start that includes multiple stakeholders; focused manageable economic efforts; strong local leadership; and economies of scale in areas such as job training, financial services, and infrastructure services (Pew Partnership for Civic Change, 2001c).

With these thoughts in mind, a small group of business people, economic developers, community developers, and artists began to talk about the future of western North Carolina and the appropriate and most productive strategy to take to create a sustainable economy. They asked themselves a very important question: What are our greatest assets? The answers surprised many of them: our people and our craft heritage. This group realized that the future would not lie in recruiting an industry that would move in and melt the worries away. Rather they realized that what had long eluded them—the industrial model—might already be in place in the form of the established "invisible factories" of craftspeople working steadily in shops, classrooms, studios, and galleries tucked away on small-town streets and back roads throughout the mountains.

The Blue Ridge Mountains have long been recognized not only for their natural beauty but also as home to functional handmade objects. The region has premier craft schools and a long legacy of decorative craft traditions, dating back to the Cherokee, the mountain traditions, the European and international craftsmen who came to the Asheville area to work on the famed Biltmore House, and the famed Bauhaus craftsmen who came to Asheville in the 1940s and established the contemporary craft movement at Black Mountain College. As HandMade's founding executive director, Becky Anderson, said, "Realizing that our future lies in our past, the challenge became apparent: Can Asheville and its surrounding mountain communities build an economy on our multimillion-dollar

asset, the 'handmade industry'"? They set out to find out. An economic impact study done by Appalachian State University discovered that the more than four thousand regional craftspeople were
generating in excess of $122 million annually: twice the cash crop of
burley tobacco (Dave and Evans, 1995). Seventy-one million dollars of that was produced by 820 crafts retailers, another $26 mil-
lion from 739 full-time craftspeople, and the final $23 million from
part-time craftspeople or those for whom craft was a second income.
In short, craft was pretty big business in the region already.

The result of these early conversations was an inclusive, region-
wide initiative called HandMade in America, an asset-driven
regional community development initiative based on craft. With
an initial implementation grant from the Pew Partnership for Civic
Change in 1993, the formal organization was launched. Over 350
people participated in the regional planning process that created
HandMade and helped determine how it could make western North
Carolina the center of handmade objects in the nation. Euphemisti-
cally and fondly called "the suits and the sandals," participants came
from all parts of the region and from all occupations. Educators,
artists, business people, tourism promoters, and concerned citizens
worked together to hammer out a product and a process that would
work for the region. Their twenty-year plan was based on six non-
negotiable principles:

1. All work is inclusive. Anyone can participate.

2. All work is done in partnership with an existing organization.

3. HandMade is regional and includes rural and urban communities as equals.

4. HandMade draws on the expertise and experience of the
   institutions in the region. It doesn't hire outside consultants
   unless mandated.

5. The particular needs and assets of communities define all
   projects.

6. HandMade in America is self-sustaining.

Over ten years in operation, HandMade has expanded and grown but never wavered from these principles. It includes thousands of craftspeople throughout the region and has initiated joint projects in education, community and economic development, environmental preservation, even brownfield reclamation using innovative approaches and existing resources. Perhaps the most extensive project HandMade has undertaken in its ten-year history is the guides to the region's craft treasures and gardens. The organization worked with citizens, artists, and small businesses throughout western North Carolina to identify places in the region that represent craft and the craft heritage. The result was the Craft Heritage Corridor—scenic drives along the Blue Ridge Parkway. These drives are featured in two books that include craft studios, galleries, and shops, as well as important historic craft schools and cooperatives, historic inns, and restaurants serving traditional mountain food. These books have been complemented with a guide to the region's gardens and farms.

Small Towns Revitalization Project

The Small Towns Revitalization Project, initiated in 1996, grew from the guidebooks. Three towns of fewer than two thousand people were disappointed that their towns had been left out. The towns felt that craft was integral to their heritage also but did not know what, if anything, they had to offer. These three small towns and a fourth that came in later approached the HandMade staff for help on cataloguing what they had and determining what they needed to do to be part of the heritage tour. As they termed it, they wanted "to put their towns on the craft heritage map." What emerged was a testament to local ingenuity and a laser focus on the assets at hand. Citizens led this effort from the beginning.

The project began with Andrews (population 1,602), Bakersville (population 357), Chimney Rock (population 175), and Mars Hill (population 1,764). A year later, two more towns joined: Robbinsville (population 747) and West Jefferson (population 1,081) (U.S. Bureau of the Census, 2000). To date, a total of twelve small towns have joined. The towns were interested for different reasons: some purely economic—getting more tourists in town, some preservation—protecting their culture and heritage from fast-food restaurants, and some community spirit—revitalizing the sense of community. In all places, these priorities were accomplished and much more. The leadership from these small towns realized that inclusion in a guidebook for the thousands of tourists who drive the Blue Ridge Parkway every year was important to their current and future economies. HandMade staff and a resource team from a neighboring town spent two and a half days in each small town, identifying and cataloging its assets—places and things that people who live there every day might miss. Based on the asset catalogue, each town created a strategic plan for the organization, design, marketing, and implementation of their collective vision for their town. They developed *sister community relationships* with other towns throughout the region that had been successful in economic development and had Main Street programs, and then, they went to work. The small towns were both revitalized and reenergized. They inspired hundreds of volunteers, restored facades and Main Streets, and most important rebuilt small communities. The results of those processes identified for the communities the great assets they had to offer. For example, in one place the community and the local college had not realized how their interests might mesh. The activities of the college—summer theater, concerts, and the like—had never really been viewed as an asset to the larger community. Another town had a close proximity to a world-famous craft school but had never connected. And finally, one had a beautiful river and river gorge that had been seen as a liability.

Chimney Rock is situated on the bluffs of the Rocky Broad River. Chimney Rock was a typical fifties or sixties mountain tourist town. The shops in town sold lots of T-shirts and rubber snakes. There was little that honored the mountain heritage or the beautiful ecological setting. The river had always been a bane to their existence: it flooded, there were huge boulders that prevented development, and it hemmed them in. "It was the road, the river, and the rock gorge." One of the reasons that Chimney Rock was so interested in the Small Towns Revitalization Project is because it needed a way to minimize the impact of the river. Six months into the revitalization process, the river reared its angry head and washed away a good portion of the town. As the rebuilding process was under way, the planning group began to think about the river as an asset, not a nuisance. When the number of visitors to Chimney Rock Park increased by 220 percent after it was transformed into a nature-based tourist venue, the village of Chimney Rock decided to pursue a nature-based approach in an attempt to entice all the new park visitors to the community. The planning group decided to build their revitalization efforts around a nature-based eco-tourism and actually bring people to the river. The committee used the river boulders to make picnic tables, they cleared brush and made pocket parks, and they created a two-mile creek walk. The problem, unfortunately, was that the town's retail revenue declined dramatically. The people drawn to eco-tourism did not want to buy rubber snakes. The change in attitude toward the river changed the town: souvenir shops became hiking stores and outdoor clothing shops; handmade crafts were reintroduced to Main Street; and town restaurants built patios overlooking the river, offered picnic baskets for tourists, and changed their color scheme from pink and purple to sage green and taupe. Business became oriented to the river—now Chimney Rock's biggest asset.

Lessons Learned: Look to the People Around You

The small-town renewal process includes eight factors that the towns and HandMade in America have identified as critical to successful renewal (Hunter and McGill, 1999):

- Self-help and accountability—helping communities help themselves
- Citizen leadership

- Building on the heritage, resources, desires, hopes and aspirations of the community

- Involvement of the whole community

- Incremental learning

- Going at the pace of the community

- Sharing stories to help citizens begin to hear and talk to one another

- Creating new and enduring partnerships

The extensive work of HandMade in America and its partners throughout the region has touched on every area that affects long-term sustainability in any kind of community—those with mountains or with asphalt. They have worked on issues such as health care for craftspeople, access to affordable capital, and job training. But most of all, they have worked from a mission that emanates from an enduring belief in people and their innate abilities and assets to create and sustain the spiritual, cultural, and community life of the region.

Neighborhood-Based Organizations

Neighborhood-based organizations are organized in a variety of forms and structures. They are sometimes supported by the city, have formal budgets to spend, and are part of a community-wide network. They can also be informal or strictly volunteer driven. Since the sixties, most cities and towns have given thought to the importance of neighborhoods individually and collectively to the health and well-being of the whole community. Neighborhood associations tend to be the most formal of neighborhood-based organizations. They are "civic organizations oriented toward maintaining and improving the quality of life in a geographically delimited residential area" (Logan and Rabrenovic, 1990, p. 68). Begun in the sixties and seventies, many by federal mandate, the formal neighborhood associations have taken different roads and different turns. According to Sirianni and Friedland (1999, pp. 57–58), there was a demand from citizens to have more direct participation in citywide decisions and governance. Some of this was in direct response to exclusive racial policies, but it was also from local and national initiatives, such as the Model Cities program and community action programs. Whatever their original impetus, neighborhood associations have evolved and developed in sustainable and effective ways.

Quasi-formal organizations such as block clubs, crime watch councils, or various kinds of booster organizations are typical. The organizational structure of these less-formal organizations can be quite casual; they often lack a title of incorporation, officers, and formal committees. They differ from other neighborhood organizations in that they are not organized for advocacy but rather take action on specific issues at various points in time (Chaskin, Brown, Venkatesh, and Vidal, 2001; Delgado, 1997).

Some neighborhood groups have functioned primarily to maintain exclusivity, whereas others are built on inclusivity and representation. The latter have formed strong partnerships and collaborations with civic groups and have evolved into citywide systems, as in Minneapolis. Despite the structure of neighborhood organizations, some activist groups are skeptical of civic-participation groups funded through local government. There is concern that these formal systems can become gatekeepers that become bureaucratic and limiting (Logan and Rabrenovic, p. 70). However, this connection to city governance, which was the topic of a ten-year study done at Tufts University, has been shown to get results. The researchers looked at five cities with well-developed associational structures—Birmingham, Alabama; Dayton, Ohio; Portland, Oregon; San Antonio, Texas; and St. Paul, Minnesota. In all five of these neighborhood systems, the federal mandates of the sixties and seventies prompted the mayors to respond to citizen demands for more participation. In each city, the system flourished because local political entrepreneurs (both in and outside city hall) enacted innovations that produced results and gained neighborhood support. Further, the structures changed the patterns of political and participatory opportunities for citizens to affect their own lives (Berry, Portnoy, and Thomson, 1993, pp. 46–70).

However, there have been some clear signals about what works and what doesn't in the development process. Neighborhood associations that have staying power seem to share five general characteristics:

1. They cover all neighborhoods, not just ones that are poor.
2. They are nonpartisan.
3. They have clear communication channels with city hall.
4. They have found their niche related to issues of influence.
5. They encourage a wide range of other forms of civic participation and connections.

Successful neighborhood associations are seen as open and trustworthy and as community builders with citizens of all income levels (Sirianni and Friedland, 1999, pp. 70–71).

The development of the neighborhood association concept has seen an evolution in impact and issues. These associations are finding themselves taking on issues, such as neighborhood safety, and services, such as parks, streets, garbage, housing, and development. Another shift in the association movement is the people involved. The factors that affect participation at the neighborhood level are driven by length of residence, protection of home values, and having children younger than five (Green and Haines, 2002, p. 72). These motivators are excellent clues for community developers as they appeal for participation. Fremont, California, has taken a new look at neighborhoods and has developed an innovative approach to their role and responsibilities. Boston, Massachusetts, has created a citywide effort to reinvigorate one of the greatest assets on neighborhood Main Streets—local commercial districts.

Fremont: It's All in the Neighborhoods

Despite the rich background of neighborhood associations, the city manager and the council in Fremont, California, wanted to avoid a bureaucratic structure that relied on the city for funding or leadership. Sister to San Francisco, Oakland, and San Jose, Fremont is the fourth largest city in the San Francisco Bay area and a relatively new kid on the block. Established as a city in 1956, Fremont was an amalgam of small farming communities that were separate entities and part of the suburban ring. Now, it has a minority majority, with 41 percent white, 37 percent Asian, 13 percent Hispanic, 3 percent African American, and 4 percent other races. It is the center of one of the largest Afghan populations in the United States (U.S. Bureau of the Census, 2000; Fremont Web site).

As a new city in the scheme of urban development, Fremont has had the luxury and the challenge of creating structures and services right the first time. Nowhere is that freshness more obvious than in the Office of Neighborhoods. Considered one of the safest cities of its size (population 208,000) in the nation, Fremont is a city of single-family homes and stable neighborhoods. However, the growth of the Silicon Valley found its way to Fremont, with a 20 percent population increase in a decade. With that change, Fremont began to experience some of the pangs of urban growth seen decades before in older communities, such as disinvestment in the older commercial areas, an increase in crime and gang activity, apartment dwellers and their neighbors at odds, and spillover from petty crime and nuisances occurring in traditionally staid neighborhoods. Wanting to turn this tide before real and irreversible problems occurred, the city manager and council created the position of *neighborhood resources manager* to initiate and coordinate a new approach to community building in Fremont. All too often, these kinds of positions go to public relations specialists—people who can spin the story, not make the story. To Fremont's credit, they hired a former community organizer whose focus was on identifying and developing grassroots leaders at the block, neighborhood, and citywide levels and strengthening their skills in basic community organizing and problem-solving techniques.

Organizers organize for the outcome they want. And in the case of Fremont and its neighborhood resource manager, Claudia Albano, the outcomes were to involve citizens, to create opportunities for them to know one another and to build relations, to develop leaders who can solve their own problems—in short, to build social capital. The city deliberately avoided the organized neighborhood association route. Although successful in many communities, too many are fraught with all the bad aspects of bureaucracy—city staff who run the meetings and set the agendas or the "usual suspects" dominating the group. Fremont wanted a system of neighborhoods that focused on action, operated on its own steam, and was not dependent on local government for either ideas or support.

In the Community Building and Engagement Initiative adopted by the city council in January 2001, key goals were identified to help the city become a place where residents

- Know one another

- Have the skills and know-how to be actively engaged in making the community better

- Work in partnership with the city to solve problems

- Support and celebrate diversity

The council approved four main strategies to accomplish these goals and invited all Fremont citizens to get more involved and connected in their community. In a city that already had in place three hundred neighborhood crime watch programs, twelve hundred community response team volunteers, and three hundred home owner associations, the question was this: What's missing? As a first strategy for the Community Building initiative, the Office of Neighborhoods saw an opportunity to build on that organizational strength in two ways: first, it wanted to strengthen the capacity of these

groups and expand their agendas to include neighborhood improvement programs, block parties, and outreach to newcomers, young
people, and seniors. Second, it wanted to join these neighborhoods
in networks across the city to encourage information sharing, networking, and problem solving.

These *neighborhood networks* are designed for the twenty-eight
neighborhood service areas. According to Albano, volunteers from
seventeen of these twenty-eight service areas have already come forward to establish the neighborhood networks. These networks are
encouraged to meet at least three times a year and to include a
broad range of citizen leaders, including neighborhood crime watch
captains; block, homeowner, and merchant associations; representatives from ethnic and cultural associations; and representatives
from the nonprofit and faith communities. Their tasks are varied
but center on information, joint projects, and social events. An
immediate undertaking is the asset mapping of their neighborhoods.

Using the process developed by Kretzmann and McKnight, residents from across the city have been trained to "map" the individual, institutional, organizational, and physical assets of their
neighborhood. Albano believes that an understanding of the glass
half full—the talents and resources in a neighborhood—refocuses
the community conversation on itself and its capacities and the
work it must do for itself. All too often, citizens give up their ownership of the community to local government—looking to it to
solve all their problems. According to Albano, identifying the assets
of a neighborhood "tweaks the minds of citizens and brings the
community back to them" in real terms. Citizens need to assume
responsibility for the health and well-being of where they live and
all the people who live there. "That's the best way for a city to work
in partnership with a neighborhood, in any case," remarked Albano,
"as peer-level partners, each with something different to contribute
to solving the problem."

The second key strategy of the Community Building and
Engagement Initiative is leadership development. This includes not
only formal leadership training but also access to available resources,

such as a special section of the Fremont Main Library devoted to videos, books, and Web sites for neighborhood leaders. It is critical, the city believes, to have a critical mass of outspoken, prepared, and visionary leaders to reinvigorate civic life.

Young people are the central component of the third strategy for community building and civic engagement. One-third of Fremont's population is under twenty-five years of age, and there are thirty-five thousand school-age children in the city. To say that today's young people are the key to Fremont's future is a great understatement. All high school students in the city are required to complete thirty hours of service learning before graduation. The plan for the third strategy is to marry that requirement with a broad set of community interests so students can get a hands-on, real-life reflective experience in their own neighborhood. This *service-learning partnership* includes a variety of community organizations and stakeholders but particularly neighborhoods where projects are easily identified and developed. In addition, the city is making volunteer opportunities for young people more visible and accessible.

The fourth strategy is aimed at technology and civic engagement, an area that fascinates and eludes so many. The Office of Neighborhoods facilitated the development of a Web site [www.fremontonline.org], now operated by a group of interested residents, that provides information and resources for Fremont's neighborhood leaders that is separate and distinct from the city's Web site. The goal was to use the asset of the 75 percent of Fremont's households having computer access to expand communication within the neighborhoods through their own Web sites or listservs. This electronic network is intended not only as an information source but also as a way to connect to others in the community.

Neighborhoods are stronger when people know one another, says Albano. There is a feeling of trust and the creation of a modern-day "backyard-fence" conversation that can be created. Neighbors knowing one another allows communities to be more social, to be safer, and to be better prepared. Albano is convinced that knowing our neighbors adds to the safety, health, and well-being of a community in good times and bad. For Fremont, this investment in neighborhoods is already bearing fruit. Citizens are getting straight talk from city hall and they are responding. As one person said, "I like the new approach of [government] working with the community." Other city departments are working out the civic-engagement dimension as they go about their work. As Albano says, "We are clear about what we want from residents. If it is input we want, we say so; if there is the possibility of partnership, we say that too."

Fremont, California, is investing in social capital and identifying assets every day through their neighborhoods program. They are preparing people with the skills they need to solve their problems, and they are connecting them in practical, modern-day ways. As Albano says, the question is not "Are they meeting?" The question is "If they need to meet, would they and could they?" That answer is getting closer and closer to yes.

Boston: What's Right on Main Street

Boston Main Streets is a public-private initiative that builds on the incredible assets of Boston's neighborhood commercial districts. This local government–initiated community and economic development program has given a "new face" to the neighborhood. In an era when shopping has gone from Main Street to megamalls to the Internet, developers, citizens, and city officials are eager to bring people and their business back to local shopping districts. These neighborhood commercial districts, once the hub for small businesses, baby carriages, and pedestrians, have seen the neighborhood core dispersed and declining. These neighborhoods, across the city, have paid a price with the decline of conveniently located retail shopping, disinvestment in infrastructure, and less opportunity for the residents to interact as part of the daily routine. Against this backdrop, Boston has found a way to revitalize local communities through building restoration, new facades, and commercial and economic revival.

Boston has found itself as a "first" over the years, including having the first public school in America. Boston has another first, however—the decision to become the first citywide Main Street program in the country. Established in 1995 by then councilman (now mayor) Thomas Menino, Boston Main Streets provides city funding and technical assistance to twenty-one neighborhood-based districts throughout the city to help these neighborhood commercial districts capitalize on their unique cultural, historical, and civic assets.

The Main Street Model was created by the National Trust for Historic Preservation in 1980 to revitalize and preserve historic or traditional commercial areas. The model ranges from strengthening civic participation, to recruiting new businesses and expanding existing ones, to rehabilitation of buildings. The work of the Main Street program builds on the inherent assets of the community. The program is in sixteen hundred communities nationally. In Boston, the twenty-one "downtowns" are restoring commercial viability and civic involvement to the areas in communities that have been hardest hit by malls, suburbs, and interstate highways.

Each participating Main Street in Boston receives funding from the city for four years through block grants and also has corporate sponsors through the "Corporate Buddy" program. In addition, the city provides six full-time staff to assist local directors with their programs. As districts throughout the city apply for participation in the program, they are asked to identify not only their financial resources but also their physical and civic assets. The districts have highlighted everything from the Liberty Tree in Chinatown; to the Eustis Street Fire House, the oldest firehouse still standing in the city in Dudley Square; to the Blessed Sacrament Church in the Hyde-Jackson district; to the home of William Trotter, the founder of the *Guardian* newspaper and the Boston Equal Rights League, in Upham's Corner.

The Boston Main Street programs identify the people, organizations, and assets that are critical for revitalization. Through the Main Street process, neighborhoods began to tally their assets as they applied for participation in the program. In Mission Hill, for example, there are seventeen civic and community organizations, twenty-eight institutions such as hospitals and educational institutions, four places of worship, and ninety businesses. Self-described as a neighborhood of black, white, and Latino—old and young—Mission Hill says that its diversity and its organization are its strengths. According to Mission Main Street director Maggie Cohn, "By working cooperatively, you get further." Technically part of Roxbury, Mission Hill is the second-highest point in the city of Boston; you can see Boston Harbor from its tip. The community was settled in the seventeenth century by German immigrants, who worked in the thirty-odd breweries that lined the local brook and the numerous tanneries. Although the breweries have long since gone, the neighborhood still retains some of the architectural remnants of the time. Perhaps one of the best-known landmarks and assets is Mission Church—the Basilica of Our Lady of Perpetual Help—whose towers frame the skyline of the community. The church has continued to keep people coming to the community for both services and school. Mission Hill is also home to the Longwood Medical Area, which includes New England Baptist Hospital, Brigham and Women's Hospital, and the Harvard Medical School among others. When asked about her community's greatest asset and the foundation of stability and development, Cohn answers, "the level of organization that residents have achieved that allows things to get done." It is the kind of community connection that Jane Jacobs (1961) described when she talked about the critical ingredient of social capital to neighborhood success. Cohn and her neighbors are finding ways to work together and develop strategies based on a great history, a broad diversity, a network of relationships, and their assets.

Emily Haber, director of Boston Main Streets, says that "the asset base of a neighborhood commercial district includes merchants, community organizations, religious institutions, hospitals, and schools but as important, the residential population that cares for and supports the district." These assets, neighborhoods have learned, were sometimes invisible to the locals. From 1995 to 2001, more than 97,153 volunteer hours were logged in the districts, the equivalent of forty-six years of full-time employee time. The capitalization and recognition of community assets are finding their way into the psyche, the visibility, and the marketing of Main Street commercial districts. Community residents are learning about and owning their heritage.

Main Street development goes beyond cultural and tourism-related development. It is about the economic revitalization of small businesses and the capturing and harnessing of local assets. The National Trust for Historic Preservation estimates that for every dollar a community spends on its local Main Street program, it leverages an additional $39.22 in new investments. In other words, building on assets *creates* assets in very tangible ways.

Lessons Learned: Building on Your Assets

These four examples—Abyssinian Development Corporation, HandMade in America (including the Small Towns Revitalization Project), Fremont, California, and Boston Main Streets—have demonstrated that building from an asset base opens new possibilities that community residents and organizations have never considered. The approach does not sugarcoat the negatives but rather places communities in a position to uncover resources that were either unused or ill-used. Kretzman and McKnight conclude their book *Building Communities from the Inside Out* (1993) with two pieces of advice. First, although outside resources are still very much needed in low-income communities, their impact will be wasted if the inside community capacity is not developed or awakened. Second, outside resources that dominate or control a community's efforts and potential will weaken the ability of the community to leverage the resources. The community must maintain a level of independence and a vision of itself.

Asset-based approaches like those profiled here do not take the place of smart public policy. They cannot make up for years of dis-investment, isolation, or lack of jobs, but they can make it possible for interventions to work when they might not otherwise. This approach can position a community and its investors to think and see differently. The cataloguing of assets is a process that leads to a product: a renewed sense of community tangibles, a start toward new relationships, and an approach that begins where people live.

Getting Started in Your Community

If this approach makes sense to you, as it does to me, the first step is to learn more about the formal process of asset mapping through Kretzmann and McKnight's book, *Building Communities from the Inside Out*. A second step is to think about your immediate neigh-borhood and the assets it has to offer. Take that a step further and think about the community at large. Third, find groups in the com-munity who could help initiate the community-wide, asset-mapping process, like the United Way, religious organizations, the chamber of commerce, or neighborhood organizations. Fourth, don't take no for an answer. Building from assets is common sense. If you start with what's right, not with what's wrong, your chances of success will go up dramatically.

5

Practicing Democracy

Whether the issue is downtown revitalization or help-
ing families, whether it is neighborhood improvement
or youth development, in every community it has
been people working together that have made these
solutions work.

Anne Ganey

Over the last decade, there has been a renewed awakening of the role of citizenship. As policies are shaped more by special interests, citizens have been pushed further and further from what Thomas Jefferson called "expressing, discussing, and deciding" the issues that they hold in common.

Framing the Issues

The purpose of this chapter is not just to extol the virtues of deliberation but rather to illustrate its practical and civic value. Deliberation among and between people in a community helps solve problems—clear and simple. In the illustrations that follow, communities have reaped the practical rewards of organizing themselves to talk and act and make choices. Dialogue provides an outlet for new ideas and creates the pathway to active problem solving.

The examples in this chapter have action as the end game. In Jacksonville, citizens know that Jacksonville Community Council Inc. is anticipating, studying, and ultimately working with others to implement thoroughly vetted solutions to some of the community's toughest problems. They also know that there is a place for their participation in the process. Through several venues in Owensboro, citizens are talking about their concerns and hearing the perspectives of others so that common strategies can be found. Some of the conversations are in formal settings; others are over a cup of coffee. The city government and citizens in Hampton have created a new way to work—*together*. Decision making is a two-way street that allows dialogue, discussion, and real input. In Wilmington, the study circles process has allowed citizens, fellow workers, nonprofit organizations, and students to talk about race openly and constructively and advance those conversations to an action agenda.

Communities that respond effectively to the problems, challenges, and opportunities that come their way have a clear understanding of democracy, both in principle and in practice. In such communities, people understand the need for active participation of a broad range and large number of ordinary citizens, not just those with formal decision-making authority. They realize that the contribution of the entire community is a practical requirement for identifying and implementing effective public policies. And they are convinced that by acting together, they can change the community or at least their part of it.

A Different Kind of Politics

There are two kinds of politics at play in communities, according to Mathews (1999). The first is found in political campaigns, voting, and political speeches. The second is found in "neighborhood associations, public forums, and organizations for civic action" (p. 122). Both are necessary for a healthy democracy. It is the second form of politics that informs the first. Democracy becomes real for people when they decide what kind of community they want, not so much which political party or candidate they support. The core of our democracy is the opportunity to discuss and decide what is in the public's interest. It is the quality and breadth of the public dialogue that provides the only avenue for changing the negative politics that have become so prevalent. It may be the lever that we need to jump-start our involvement in politics and affect our own destiny.

The civic goal, then, is both to prepare people to act as responsible citizens and to carve out ways that meaningful participation is feasible and possible. Hannah Pitkin contends that the public must see public discourse and deliberation as part of its role and responsibility as citizens and not as an option to be pursued by the leisure class. It is the process by which citizens determine how they will live together and create the future (1981, p. 343). Politics and public life then go far beyond voting, as Mathews, Pitkin, and others argue, and it must include the interaction of citizens to make choices—usually difficult choices. This opportunity to make informed, rational decisions in concert with a community of fellow citizens provides the interconnectedness that is often lost in society. The issues that often need us most elude our ability to discuss and decide.

Public dialogue, as opposed to public debate, provides the opportunity to join with others to learn, discuss, and understand multiple perspectives. This dialogue enlivens democracy, but it also allows a better chance for problems to be solved and opportunities to be met. As William Sullivan observes, "Public discussion brings before the whole community an understanding of the 'externalities' of public choices . . . that is, what certain choices mean for certain groups" (1982, p. 166). There is concern, however, that the "public" is no longer easy to find or even in existence. The public is viewed as a collection of individuals out for their own gain. A recent national survey, however, found a public ready to connect for things bigger than their own interests.

A Willing Public

In order to understand the potential impact of the deliberative process, it is important to know the public's willingness to act on new information and new perspectives. A survey commissioned by the Pew Partnership for Civic Change in 2003, *What Will It Take? Making Headway on Our Most Wrenching Problems*, shows that America is brimming with individuals who are ready and willing to get involved in improving the quality of life in their communities. The survey results depict the public as a largely untapped resource whose collective skills and enthusiasm could profitably be brought to bear to address persistent problems such as hunger, illiteracy, and neighborhood safety. Clearly, one of the greatest benefits of citizen involvement is that it can help alleviate community problems. But in addition, citizen participation can promote community dialogue and connectedness and can give citizens a sense of efficacy—a feeling that their efforts matter and can make a difference. The challenge for community organizations lies in knowing how to connect community problems with a public willing to work to solve them. Public dialogue and discussion make this possible.

Recognizing That a Problem Is a Problem

Citizens must overcome two barriers to greater civic involvement, according to the survey. First, many citizens are unaware of the nature and seriousness of problems in their communities. When asked whether affordable housing, hunger, neighborhood safety, illiteracy, and quality of public education were problems in their communities, significant numbers of respondents said no or not much of one. In particular, majorities of respondents believed that hunger (72 percent), illiteracy (66 percent), and the quality of public education (68 percent) were not a problem or not much of a problem in their communities. These perceptions belie the national statistics on all of these issues. Community dialogue can be a vehicle for educating the public on critical issues.

A second barrier to participation for many people was that they are unsure of whom to contact to get involved in their communities. Thirty-five percent of those surveyed said that not knowing whom to call is a reason why they have not gotten involved in their community.

Communities cannot involve citizens in addressing major challenges or opportunities if citizens do not believe these to be problems in the first place. Interestingly, even though much of the public does not see many social issues as problems in their own communities, a majority believes that there is much they could do to solve many of these problems if they were recognized as such. For instance, although only a small minority of survey respondents view hunger as a serious problem locally, 81 percent believe that people like themselves can help solve the problem of hunger in their community. Seventy-one percent said the same about illiteracy, and 54 percent said the same about public education. Despite the public's optimistic view of the seriousness of community problems, survey respondents display a willingness to help and a faith in the efficacy of their work if there is a problem.

One reason the public may not fully grasp the seriousness of community problems is that they are not exposed to or do not seek information that translates the extent of these problems to their own backyards. Political scientists have found that whereas people tend to praise *their* member of Congress or local school, they often distrust or criticize the institution of Congress or public education generally. Perhaps the same dynamic is at work here: people recognize hunger, housing, and the quality of public education as problems at the national level but do not see how these issues affect their own communities.

Getting the Right Information

Although it may be hard to believe that people don't have enough information in the era of information deluge, I believe that the public gets too much or not enough of what they really need. Issues are too often presented as "snapshots," not the whole portfolio.

This lack of knowledge on issues provides an opportunity for nonprofit organizations, community groups, and local governments to join with the public to learn more about the challenges the community is facing and to provide forums in which people can get involved in addressing them. It provides an opportunity for the public to take responsibility for being informed. It is a two-way street. Community groups can tap into the public's enthusiasm and willingness to help by raising the visibility of the work that they do. By providing more information via the sources the public uses to get its information about community issues, nonprofit organizations can inform the public about local problems and reach out to potential volunteers, rather than expecting volunteers to discover what the community needs on their own. As we will see later, this is exactly the strategy that the communities profiled in this chapter have adopted, with great success.

When asked about their main source for news and information about what's going on in the community, 37 percent of survey respondents mentioned television and 28 percent mentioned the daily newspaper. In addition, 28 percent of respondents believe that a local newspaper or newsletter is the most direct way for people to find out about opportunities to volunteer, followed closely by neighbors or word of mouth (17 percent) and television (11 percent). These findings offer a blueprint for community and nonprofit leaders interested in encouraging civic activism in the issues they champion.

In order for people to participate in community problem solving, they need to know where to turn for information about the community's needs. In addition, as more individuals become involved, word of mouth becomes a more powerful and effective recruiting device. Learning about what is going on in the community through a public forum and how their skills could be put to use gives citizens the relationships and tools to become more involved in community life.

Findings from a companion survey of nonprofit executives demonstrate that there is a disconnect in how people "in the trenches" view community problems versus how the public views them. Still, findings from both surveys suggest that as nonprofit organizations and the public learn what they need from one another, the prospects for civic activism and community problem solving will improve.

The Pew Partnership survey findings paint an optimistic picture of the public's role in community life, albeit one with some important nuances. Large numbers of people say they are willing to be more engaged in tackling tough community issues together. Nonprofit organizations and local governments have the opportunity to see the public as a willing and enthusiastic partner in efforts to solve local problems. Communities and groups can better engage the public by finding ways to inform them about the seriousness of the issues in their own backyards, by making the public more aware of community needs through the information sources that the public relies on the most, and by providing forums through which the public can apply its talents and resources to tackling critical challenges. With a better grasp of the skills that the public has to offer, community challenges can be joined with available resources in order to facilitate problem-solving efforts and bring citizens more fully into the lives of their communities.

Can We Talk?

Communities often have no place, space, or convenor that allows for citizens to come together. The avenues for participation too often come in formal public meetings, fiery special-interest sessions, or the morning breakfast group conversation at the local diner. These all have their place, but there must be vehicles for regular, ongoing dialogue that has currency with people. We need opportunities that allow citizens to do more than just talk, but rather talk, decide, and do.

So where do citizens turn when they want to participate? The formation of this public system of democracy can begin in local libraries, in nonprofit organizations, through regional agencies, through historical associations, or in city hall—any organization that can provide information and a public space for people to practice politics. Citizens want to and must know how to deliberate and act on the issues important to them. The first step in this process is to convene.

The places profiled in this chapter bear out many of the themes that the survey respondents articulated. First, in these communities evidence shows that education, dialogue, and deliberation can make the public more aware of the seriousness of local problems and can provide a catalyst for addressing those problems. In turn, greater public involvement may encourage a *culture of collaboration*, which not only solicits citizen participation but also encourages and expects it. In turn, the public requests and accepts responsibility for helping solve community challenges. At its best, community problem solving can harness the energy and enthusiasm of citizens working together, putting their talents to work to address problems, and at the same time promote a sense of ownership over the processes and outcomes of democratic community life.

In addition, we will see in this chapter that these four communities have confronted precisely the barriers to civic activism that the survey identified: a lack of awareness of the seriousness of problems in the community and an uncertainty about whom to contact to get involved in solving those problems. These communities have provided a forum for civic activism through which citizens work together to identify, understand, and solve pressing problems.

Jacksonville: Knowing What We Need to Know

During the 1960s, community leaders and elected officials of Jacksonville, Florida, began to realize that a number of serious problems facing the city could only be addressed effectively with widespread support from the community. The city was poised to enter a period of tremendous physical growth and development. Community leaders and citizens alike questioned the city's readiness for the future and its ability to respond to the challenges that the inevitable changes would bring. In 1974, the president-elect of the Jacksonville Area Chamber of Commerce convened a three-day planning meeting for a hundred civic leaders from the city and Duval County, including public officials, city council members, labor representatives, military personnel, religious leaders, and top-level business executives. At a pivotal time in Jacksonville's history, representatives from a fragmented community with diverse sectional interests came together and talked about Jacksonville, its problems, and its opportunities. The participants created a priority list of critical issues facing the community and developed a shared commitment to solve the identified problems. Further, the participants agreed that there needed to be a mechanism for continuing the dialogue begun at the conference. The result was the decision to establish the Jacksonville Community Council Inc. (JCCI), a nonprofit, broad-based civic organization that began operation in 1975. JCCI expanded its scope in subsequent years to include all facets of the community. It is both a planning council and a civic league: a hybrid mission that allowed JCCI to study, deliberate, and act on issues of greatest concern, with citizens playing the major role. As former mayor John Delaney says, "JCCI has a twenty-seven-year history of working with citizens to develop practical solutions to community challenges. Whether it's studying the homeless issue, exploring the racial divide, or developing solutions to visual pollution, JCCI has been in the forefront of improving our quality of life by seeking conscience on public policy matters. When JCCI analyzes an issue and makes recommendations, things happen."

JCCI "makes things happen" by organizing and administering two continuing activities that play a key role in improving life in the Jacksonville area. One is the annual publication of *Quality of Life Indicators*—reports that assess the state of the economy, education, the environment, public safety, health, and other matters vital to the quality of life for Jacksonville area residents. These are considered a primary source for alerting the community to problems and opportunities.

The second activity is the formation and guidance of two annual citizen-based *study committees*, which are charged with responsibility for fully, fairly, and accurately exploring an important issue of community concern. The task for each committee is to analyze the issue carefully, to ascertain the facts involved, and to ensure that it is examined from multiple points of view.

The study committee process begins in the spring. The JCCI board identifies two problems or issues for study. The president of the board then selects a volunteer to chair the study committee meetings. In turn, the chair chooses members of a volunteer management team to help shepherd the process. Over the summer, JCCI staff do background research on the problem or issue and work with the chair and management team to develop a calendar of weekly meetings. In September, through its newsletter and through press releases and public service announcements, JCCI solicits volunteers from the community to serve on the committees. "We don't want only people who are stakeholders in the issue," comments Lois Chepenik, executive director of JCCI. "We want impartial people in the community who come with a blank slate, who just want to learn about the issues and form their own opinions as they hear more about it" (Dusack, 2000, p. 33). Sixty to one hundred people typically sign up to participate in a study committee.

Study committees typically range in size from about 30 to more than 150 persons, depending on the topic being studied and the ability of participants to commit a minimum of ninety minutes of their time per week over a six- to eight-month period. Because the credibility of a committee's report depends on the credibility of the committee's makeup, JCCI pays careful attention to the need for the committee to represent the diversity of the community at large.

Every effort is made and vehicle used to get the word out so that citizens from all walks of life and all demographic categories are well represented on the study committees.

Each of the committee's roughly two dozen meetings is facilitated by the volunteer chair, a person who is well regarded throughout the community but who is not involved or identified with the matter under consideration. The chair has responsibilities for both the process and the content of the study. *Process responsibilities* include ensuring that committee members listen closely and actively to the information presented to them, that persons appearing before the committee provide it with information to address the questions they have been given beforehand, that committee members pose their own questions and interact constructively, and that staff assistance is adequate and appropriate. The chair's *content responsibilities* include ensuring that proper planning is done, that the study problem or issue is covered thoroughly in the fact-finding sessions, that it is examined from multiple points of view, and that the report accurately and adequately reflects the committee's findings, conclusions, and recommendations.

The first fifteen or so meetings of the study committee are devoted to producing a set of factual *findings*. This *joint learning* is crucial to the study committee process in at least two respects:

- First, it ensures that committee members enter into the decision-making phase of the process with a shared knowledge base. When committee members have reached consensus on the facts, they are, in the words of one JCCI staff person, "more than 90 percent of the way home." Joint learning ensures as well that when the findings are released to the general public, members of the public will treat the facts reported to them as thoroughly investigated, well documented, and hence, as completely reliable and beyond dispute.

• Second, the collective study of factual questions by committee members affords them their first practical lesson in consensual decision making, a skill they will need in subsequent phases of the process.

In the second phase of the process—the next three to four meetings—committee members work toward a consensus regarding *conclusions*—a set of shared value-based judgments based on the findings. In the third phase of the committee's deliberations— the last three to five meetings—members consensually develop *recommendations*—a set of action steps for the community to take that will be included in the committee's written *report* to the community.

When the study committee has finished its work, the chair, aided by the committee, presents the report to the JCCI Board of Directors for review and approval. Once approved by the board, the content of the report becomes the official position of JCCI. It is released to the community at a public event in late spring—about a year after the problem or issue was approved by the board for study.

Finally, in the *implementation stage*, community volunteers, who frequently include members of the study committee, spend the following two years educating individuals and organizations about the findings and conclusions and urging them to act on the committee's recommendations.

The JCCI study process drew on the model developed by the Citizens League of Minnesota, which had developed a consensus-based approach to public decision making. As generally understood, *consensus* means that all who have participated in a group's discussions can live with—or go along with—the conclusions the group reaches. It does not mean complete agreement. Nor does it mean that participants are equally satisfied with—or enthusiastic about— the result. But it does mean that they recognize that the result is the best one for the community as a whole and the best that practically can be achieved.

After almost three decades of JCCI's existence, a distinctive JCCI model of citizen-based consensual decision making has emerged. Among other things, the model is unique in its successful blending of citizen-based consensual decision making with the technical, financial, and logistical strengths of organizational human services planning. Since 1977, there have been sixty-two citizen studies conducted.

The reports of JCCI study committees have led directly to a number of beneficial changes in the Jacksonville area, including the following:

- In response to a study on teen pregnancy, an innovative youth center, the Bridge of Northeast Florida, was established to assist young people in making better life choices.

- A human services council, now in its twentieth year, was established, which brings together all regional private and public funders of health services, enabling them to leverage resources for health and other human services.

- An economic development incentives policy was adopted for the City of Jacksonville.

- A city charter referendum to regulate and remove billboards was approved by the public.

- A communities-in-schools program was adopted.

- A partnership-for-workforce preparation was formed.

- City contracts for minority-owned businesses increased.

- A community agenda report, covering a wide range of health and human services issues for the five-county region of Northeast Florida, is released annually.

- There has been an unprecedented level of constructive public discussion concerning race relations.

- Perhaps the most significant achievement of all has been the *Quality of Life Indicators* assessment. Created in Jacksonville, it was the first of its kind and is now used in more than a thousand communities throughout the United States and the world.

JCCI estimates that the recommendations contained in study committee reports are fully or partially implemented *between 80 and 85 percent of the time*. Even more important, JCCI's efforts have fostered the growth of a civic culture in Jacksonville in which citizens now *expect* that they will participate in, contribute to, and exercise real influence over any key decision made by municipal government. As a result of being made a full partner in governing their community, citizens have been willing to take greater responsibility for solving the problems and addressing the issues confronting Jacksonville. In 2000, for example, voters overwhelmingly approved an increase in the sales tax to generate revenue for downtown capital improvements. JCCI's efforts have helped residents of the Jacksonville area to understand, appreciate, and embrace citizen-driven, consensus-based decision making.

JCCI sustains citizen interest through continual citizen participation in identifying problems or issues to be studied, obtaining and analyzing data concerning them, and refining indicators that illuminate the quality of life that currently prevails in the community. There is always more work to be done.

JCCI is working on new ways to involve younger citizens and members of the African American community in the civic life of the community. JCCI recognizes that it must work on two community fronts simultaneously: the level of the region and the level of the neighborhood. Bringing citizen-driven, consensus-building principles and practices to these arenas represents the next frontier for JCCI's pioneering efforts. Finally, JCCI has launched an initiative, JCCI Forward, which identifies emerging leaders and prepares them to take a more active role in community change (Dusack, 2000, p. 34).

Other communities have organized themselves around a specific issue or set of issues, and that initial start has led to a range of other discussions. Owensboro, Kentucky; Hampton, Virginia; and Wilmington, Delaware, have created avenues for citizens to come to the table, but just as important, to create opportunities to take that collective knowledge and make short-term and long-term change.

Owensboro: Creating a Constituency for Change

In Owensboro, Kentucky, the community has been literally talking to itself for the last six years. Public deliberation is becoming a way of doing business in the community. Several organizations are taking the lead in making that happen: the Public Life Foundation, Community Conversations, Inc., and the Conversation Café. The first National Issues Forums (NIF) were held in Owensboro in late 1998 on the topic of "Kids Who Commit Crime." Since then, the community has used NIF, study circles, and their own issue framing to talk about issues such as access to health care, land use planning, and citizens and law enforcement. These early experiences led to more formal and wider-spread adoption of deliberative forums.

Lack of access to high-quality affordable health care is a major problem for many Americans today, particularly in the smaller towns and rural areas of the country. Recognizing this need, more than twenty organizations decided to sponsor a comprehensive health needs assessment in 2000 for a seven-county area surrounding and including Owensboro, an Ohio River city of fifty-four thousand, in the western part of the state, the third largest city in the state. Two major themes emerged from the assessment conducted by the University of Kentucky (UK), both of them barriers to a healthier citizenry: *limited access to health care* and *unhealthy lifestyles*.

In Owensboro and Daviess County, a number of organizations were already focusing on the lifestyle issues raised by the UK report. But no one was focusing on impediments to health care access. This prompted the Public Life Foundation of Owensboro to take the initiative in stimulating public discussion on the access problem. According to Rodney Berry, president of the foundation, this spurred the creation of the People's Health Project to provide an opportunity for citizens from all parts of the community to identify their chief concerns and priorities and to gauge the kinds of action steps the community would be most inclined to support.

With the aid of input from a citizen advisory committee, the Public Life Foundation prepared public discussion guides for seven issues related to access to health care and organized fifty-two forums (small-group discussions) throughout the city and county between March 2001 and February 2002. All forums were opened to the public and were promoted in the newspaper, in organization bulletins, and on posters and fliers. Realizing, however, that simply opening forums to the public would not, by itself, ensure widespread participation from citizens representing the diversity of the population, the foundation enlisted community groups—churches, neighborhood associations, civic and service clubs, professional and trade associations, and so forth—to reach out to potential participants who collectively would constitute a cross section of the community. More than 1,100 people received personal invitations. These efforts attracted 578 participants to the forums, an average of just over 11 persons per forum.

Drawing on local data and information, the discussion guides helped frame the health care–access challenges identified in the UK study. For each challenge, supporting data were suppliedand key issues were identified. The organizers worked hard to design discussion booklets that would be compelling to participants and that would lead to discussions relevant to the prospects for local action. They took great care as well to craft the booklets in a way that rendered them accurate, balanced, and easy to understand.

Drawing on proven models for citizen deliberation of tough public issues, such as study circles and the National Issues Forums, the organizers constructed their own unique format for deliberation. Trained facilitators helped participants carry on their forum discussions, which generally lasted from two to two and a half hours.

In the view of organizers, the People's Health Project forums have heightened recognition by both the general public and community leaders that limited access to health care is a serious problem in Owensboro and Daviess County. They believe that a number of initiatives undertaken by groups would not have happened as quickly or might not have occurred at all had it not been for the People's Health Project assessment and forums. For example, they cite the following:

- Upon learning that one-fourth of the adults in Daviess County do not have a regular doctor and hence use the local hospital emergency room to obtain their primary care, the hospital added a social worker in the emergency room to help patients connect with a primary care provider. The hospital also funded a full-time physician to work in a free clinic.

- Daviess County government applied for and received a $2 million federal grant to address health care access.

- The hospital, health department, and county government are collaborating on crafting a comprehensive health access initiative modeled after the Buncombe County, North Carolina, Project Access program.

Since the forums, the Public Life Foundation of Owensboro has taken action as well. For example, they have done the following:

- Published the community's first *Primary Care Directory and Resource Guide to Community Health Centers*

- Commissioned a prescription drug study and convened and facilitated the work of a prescription drug task force that developed a prescription drug–service center model

- Commissioned a study on health care costs, with a particular interest in examining why health care costs and insurance premiums are higher in the Owensboro-Daviess County area than in most other areas of Kentucky

- Convened, helped organize, and provided staff and administrative support for the community's first grass-roots health care coalition: Citizens Health Care Advocates (CHCA)

The CHCA was a group of interested, engaged citizens from the People's Health Project forums. Formed in 2002, the CHCA now has more than eighty members and has attracted more than three hundred different citizens to its monthly meetings.

The foregoing actions resulted from the efforts of the Owensboro-Daviess County community to come together to address a problem. The early success of Citizens Health Care Advocates reflects the growth of a constituency for improvements in health care that did not exist previously or at least had not yet mobilized. CHCA members are increasingly informed and engaged, and they have a genuine sense of ownership in their organization. They have the courage to speak out and to raise important questions.

In another community, public deliberation might have come to an end with the conclusion of the People's Health Project forums. But that was not the case in Owensboro. At about the same time that the project was being organized, another group of community leaders was participating in a twenty-month-long partnership with the Kettering Foundation in Dayton, Ohio. In mid-2000, members of this group established Community Conversations, Inc. (CCI) with the aim of identifying and developing an inclusive, deliberative process that would aid the citizens of Owensboro in exploring and discussing important public issues. The purpose of the organization is to offer citizens a neutral, safe place to listen and learn from one another while talking in a civil manner about matters of shared concern.

CCI's first forums were built around issues books that had been prepared for use by citizens across the country who participate in National Issues Forums. The first issue for which CCI organized forums addressed questions of land use, then later, they held a forum to discuss the racial tension that had flared up in response to a police shooting. Not long after these forums, a local hotel owner's interest in opening a casino made legalized gambling an issue. CCI's forums stimulated an intense community-wide discussion, evidenced by a flood of letters to the local newspaper and by the spontaneous emergence of additional forums.

Although CCI was having success with the National Issues Forums model, the organization's board members saw a need for the community to find a way to frame and deliberate on issues unique to Owensboro. They believed that citizens needed a way to continue talking with one another over a longer period of time than a single two- or three-hour forum affords and not to be restricted to a predetermined set of choices. Moreover continued discussion would enable participants to work through the feelings, whether mixed or strongly held, that the issue evoked and to delve more deeply into it. Participants also needed to find ways that they might act, individually or together, in response to their findings and conclusions.

The approach of the Study Circles Resource Center in Pomfret, Connecticut, was especially well suited for these requirements. Accordingly, CCI began relying on this process to promote inclusive, deliberative discussion throughout the community. As Kathy Christie, CCI executive director, observes, "Public deliberations are the track every community needs to be on. But there are lots of different cars on the train moving in that direction." "All that matters," she says, "is that there be many opportunities for citizens to talk in settings where they are comfortable, welcome, free to express their own views, and open to hearing and considering the views of others." Ultimately, "It's about creating new habits and a new way of life, about changing the culture of our community—not just for those who live here now, but for future generations as well."

CCI continues to search for and to experiment with new ways to turn Owensboro into one large multivocal continuing conversation. For example, with CCI backing, a board member is taking the lead in exploring the possibility of "coffee house conversations." An employee of a state agency with a background in community sociology, Chad Gesser, believes that public deliberation needs to become almost an everyday experience for the citizens of Owensboro. That is the idea behind the Conversation Café—a flexible, informally structured opportunity for a small group of persons, usually five to six, to spend an hour or two talking about an issue of current interest. Topics are posted, and all are welcome. This civic experiment is essential, according to Gesser, for improving public-oriented communication among the citizens of Owensboro, for building their civic relationships, and for making public deliberation a routine part of Owensboro's way of life. The concept is being used in cities around the country (www.conversationcafe.org) to give citizens a place to talk and listen.

Christie is persuaded that Community Conversations, Inc. has already succeeded in changing the culture of public discussion in Owensboro. For example, she notes that public meetings are being conducted much differently than they were previously. They are more constructive, less rancorous, more inclusive, and much more accepting of the contribution that ordinary citizens can make to sound decision making. "The difference is between light and dark," she remarks. In addition, "There are just a lot more places where this kind of conversation is occurring. It's not always as deliberative or as well structured as it might be, but it's still valuable. It's citizens talking to each other, learning new ways to communicate, building better relationships, and in the process, changing the culture of our community."

Hampton: Local Government as a Listener

The citizens of Hampton, Virginia, have been, for more than fifteen years, the beneficiary—and partner—of a city government that both grasps and puts into practice the basic truth that democratic government must not be just for the people, but of them and by them as well.

In 1987, the City of Hampton's proposed General Plan Update (of its 1977 plan) provoked intense opposition from neighborhood groups in the northern part of the city. Citizens were irate because the update included a plan to build a new east-west freeway to relieve traffic on a major thoroughfare, for which projected increases in traffic volume pointed to a severe traffic crisis within the next ten to fifteen years. An even more important reason for the anger of neighborhood associations in the area was that they had not been consulted about how to deal with the traffic problem, and in particular, about the proposed freeway solution.

In many respects, Hampton's experience in 1987 was typical of the way many municipal governments in American cities have tried to solve problems historically. The usual procedure has been for city planners to analyze the problem, develop options, choose the best solution from among them, and present it to city council for approval. Sometimes public hearings are held to receive citizen comments on the proposed solution. But seldom does such input have a substantial impact on the plan that has already been developed.

Hampton's response was anything but typical, however. Bob O'Neill, city manager at the time, held a meeting with the neighborhood groups and proposed that they join city government in a consensus-based process to produce a new plan that would generate a solution acceptable to everyone. The neighborhood associations agreed.

City staff and representatives of the neighborhood associations agreed on a list of stakeholders and formed an *initiating committee*, consisting of representatives from four neighborhood groups, three business groups, and three members of city staff. The assistant city manager was selected to serve as facilitator. The committee met weekly for four months, during which time they set the ground rules for the consensus process. After agreeing on the rules and participants in the process, the committee took its proposal to a large group of stakeholders, who approved it at a public meeting. Finally, a working committee was assembled, comprising the members of the initiating committee, the chair of the planning commission, a representative of the affected business interests, and two at-large citizens from other areas of the city.

Beginning in late 1988, the working committee held a three-hour meeting every week or two. All meetings were open and were well covered by a local newspaper. When ideas or suggestions were made, neighborhood groups and others were invited to attend the meetings of the committee. After a year, the working committee produced a plan that most people agreed was not only acceptable but actually better than the one proposed originally by the city.

Just a few years later, the city took the initiative to apply its collaborative model to the topic of public education. The question quickly became one of healthy youth development more generally. The result was the establishment of a youth coalition and a strategic plan for youth development.

The success of the 1987 General Plan Update and the subsequent youth development initiative set off a wave of changes during the 1990s in the way the City of Hampton works, and in the way it relates to the community it serves. According to the assistant city manager, Mike Monteith, a thirty-year veteran of Hampton City government, among citizens "there is now a pervasive expectation of collaboration on almost every important matter." Results from the process include the following:

- With extensive assistance from city staff, new neighborhood associations were formed and developed. City staff helps them build organizational capacity, acquire skills ranging from community organizing to mediation, and find resources for projects and programs.

- The city formed the Neighborhood Commission, which is composed of representatives of neighborhoods in ten newly created districts.

- The city established the Neighborhood Office and appointed a full-time director so that there would be an entity that would have as its primary purpose sustaining and enhancing collaboration with citizens. The Neighborhood Office now has its work supported by other department employees and community volunteers.

- City government as a whole—not just the Planning Department—has adopted collaborative decision making as a way of doing business. There is now a deeply rooted *culture of collaboration* within city government.

- Citizens have a positive view of city government and the way it conducts its business. Distrust of the city has greatly diminished. Citizens feel empowered.

- A large and growing number of citizens have participated in consensus-based interactions with city staff. Many have taken advantage of opportunities the city provides (such as the Neighborhood College) to increase their knowledge of city government and to develop their own collaborative skills. As a consequence, Hampton's pool of community leaders has expanded dramatically. Over the past fifteen years, several citizens have received the inspiration and acquired the skills needed in order to run for and be elected to city council. Their presence on the council has helped generate and sustain political support for the enormous amount of time and energy that city staff put into engaging in and enhancing collaboration with the community.

- More generally, the city's commitment to involving as many citizens as possible in collaborative decision making has helped build a stronger sense of community. A community spirit has emerged that has enabled and encouraged citizens to feel real ownership of their neighborhoods, their community, and their city government. It's important to note that along with this sense of ownership has come an acceptance by citizens of responsibility for helping solve the problems and meet the challenges their neighborhoods and community face. Citizens in Hampton today are much less disposed than previously to ask what city government can do for them. Instead they ask how they can work with government to get things done.

Hampton's commitment to collaborative decision making is both broad and deep. The commitment of both the community and city government to collaborative problem solving seems unshakable and is likely to thrive well into the future. To some degree, Hampton has become a victim of its own success. The enthusiasm that citizens have shown for participating collaboratively in the decisions that affect them has placed an immense demand on city resources, stretching city staff to the limits of their time and energy. The challenge is compounded by the fact that, as Monteith observes, "Government is getting harder every year." The problems are bigger, the issues are more complex, and the needs of people are more pressing. Although Hampton's culture of collaboration has helped it cope better than many communities with the pressures generated by contemporary conditions, city officials realize that they must be able to do more and do it more efficiently.

Hampton city officials are—in the best sense of the term—"true believers" in and unwavering advocates for the principles and practices of citizen-government collaboration. Still, to other communities that wish to emulate what Hampton has accomplished, they offer words of caution. Everyone must accept that citizen-government collaboration is often a messy, slow, uncertain, and resource-intensive way to conduct a community's business. No city should undertake to adopt it unless government is fully committed to it from the outset. All elements of city government must be on board. In particular, there must be political support from elected officials.

Moreover both citizens and city staff must be prepared to learn from one another and to grow together. Citizens and city officials alike must see results and enjoy successes right from the beginning. Failed attempts at collaboration can be worse than not making the attempt at all, because there is nothing worse than raising expectations and then not delivering on them.

Finally, city officials in Hampton realize that by empowering citizens, they are unleashing an enormously powerful force. Once in its embrace, there is no letting go. As Joan Kennedy, Hampton's Neighborhood Office director, observes, "It's like dancing with a bear—you don't stop unless the bear wants to."

Wilmington: Getting Race Relations on the Table and into Talk

Delaware is an interesting state. The last stop on the Underground Railroad, it is one of the smallest states, with only three counties. Because of its size, many traditional services handled at the local or county level in larger states are delivered by Delaware state government. Likewise an activity or program in one county or in one of the major cities is likely to have statewide impact, as was the case with the Study Circles on Race and Racism held first in Wilmington.

The YWCA in New Castle County, Delaware, which encompasses Wilmington, the largest city at 73,135, is more than a hundred years old. Its centennial birthday in 1995 marked a decision that would set the community on a new path. The YWCA began convening organizational partnerships to work for social change. Initially, their focus in Wilmington and in Delaware was local implementation of the national YWCA's Week Without Violence. Their quick success, combined with their national priority of eliminating racism, their birthday celebration, their need and desire to promote more partnerships in the community, created the opportunity to get the community talking about the issues of violence and race. Joining with partners from the U.S. Attorney's Office and domestic violence–prevention groups, the YWCA and their new partners invited groups of citizens from across the community to talk about the issue. At the conclusion of those discussions, the YWCA approached their partners about continuing the dialogue in some fashion. According to YWCA executive director Ruth Sokolowski, "We didn't have a way in the community for the average citizen to talk with others about common concerns." On whether to continue with either violence or racism, the group of partners had differing opinions. Some felt that racism was the fundamental issue in all discussions, and other issues could not get a fair hearing without starting there. Another group felt that race was the "divider" issue, and that citizens would not come to such discussions. The partners settled their opposing views by all participating in a racism conversation based on a discussion guide prepared by the Study Circles Resource Center, an independent, nonprofit organization based in Pomfret, Connecticut. After the study circle conversations, the group, almost unanimously, decided that race was the place to begin.

Most of the original partners, and others that joined later, began the process of holding forums, training additional facilitators, and creating action steps. The YWCA continued as the lead organizer of the partnership. The community-wide emphasis on the elimination of racism was a logical extension and application of the YWCA's local and national mission. The partners also decided to stay with the study circle process as their primary vehicle for convening (www.studycircles.org).

The newly formed study circle partnership in Wilmington began officially in 1997 with seven hundred people participating and seventy-five partner organizations committing volunteers, publicity, financial and in-kind support, and meeting space. In the last six years, participation has grown to over seventy-five hundred throughout the state, with more than a hundred partners on board. The original target population of "average citizen" participation has been expanded to include workforce groups, faith-based organizations, and students and adults from schools. More than 250 citizens have been trained as study circle facilitators.

The partners have carved out specific roles that they can best play based on their organizational mission. For example, the State Human Relations Commission trains the facilitators, the National Conference of Community and Justice works with the schools, and the State Office of Personnel coordinates the outreach with state agencies. Others, like the Dupont Corporation, commit both money and corporate commitment to the process for its internal application as well as for the community work.

At the conclusion of the first year of study circles, organizers realized that participants wanted to take the next step—moving from dialogue to action. Action groups were established so that participants could continue their work in areas of common interest. Early action groups included Reaching Our Children, Deepening Our Knowledge, and Study Circles Recruitment. Their action steps range from organizing more study circles, to sponsoring programs within schools, to creating cultural festivals, and to developing information sources for the media. A partner organization, the Retired and Senior Volunteer Program, prepared an *Action Guide* to assist groups and individuals in joining together on specific action and to identify opportunities in the community to address racism directly.

Study Circles on Racism have found a variety of homes in the greater Wilmington community, extending down the state to Sussex and Kent Counties, but also neighboring Aberdeen Proving Grounds in Maryland, and West Chester, Pennsylvania. The biggest workplace application of study circles in the nation occurred in Delaware with more than four hundred Department of Labor employees participating in 1998. Elected officials, including the mayor of Wilmington and the governor, have embraced and supported study circles. The State Department of Education gives in-service training credit to teachers who participate in study circles. High schools have student-led study circles.

The process of deciding has given citizens and partner organiza-tions both the experience and the vehicle to talk about issues. The program has become a platform for inclusive, collaborative work on other social issues. Why do people in Wilmington and throughout the state give up ten hours or more of their time to talk about race? According to Sokolowski, "They want a place to have an honest, open conversation about racism."

Lessons Learned: Why Is "Talk" Important?

These communities have responded to a need of citizens to find their place in the public policy process. As Berry, Portnoy, and Thomson write in *The Rebirth of Urban Democracy* (1993), "Rebuilding citizenship in America means that reform of voting must move beyond getting people into private voting booths to get-ting more people to public forums where they can work with their neighbors to solve the problems of their communities" (p. 2). They believe that in order to move beyond adversarial politics, "where interest groups square off in conflict and lobbyists speak for their constituents," citizens must join together to identify problems and look for common solutions (p. 3).

When Robert Bellah and his colleagues wrote *Habits of the Heart* (1985), they found a trend toward individualism, to be sure, but they also found a profound need by Americans to be involved. A study, *Citizens and Politics: A View from Main Street America*, in the early 1990s by the Harwood Group (1991) for the Kettering Foun-dation found similarly that Americans could not find their place in public life, not because they are apathetic as the common wisdom holds, but because they were politically impotent. That is, they felt unable to make any difference at all in public decisions.

The form of participating democracy that the communities pro-filed here are practicing can be both redemptive and programmatic. Connection with others nourishes and encourages the human spirit. Connection also creates a sense of community among participants. It transforms institutions into new ways of operating. Research on dialogue by Daniel Yankelovich (1999) and William Isaacs (1999) has shown the transformative power of dialogue. It can be a healer, but more important, it opens the minds and hearts of the speakers and the listeners to a new realm of thinking and acting.

For example, the type of dialogue created and the methods used by the Jacksonville Community Council Inc. are transferable to and usable in any community, whatever its composition, character, problems, and issues. A key to that organization's success has been to avoid the trap of relying solely on a few highly motivated and involved citizens to get things done. It is imperative, they believe, to create a genuine public forum in which all citizens can participate and contribute. They also urge other communities not to neglect the hard work of implementing the recommendations that citizens have produced. Without evidence that consensus-building deliberation works, that it is effective in bringing about needed change, citizens eventually will lose faith in this approach to democratic self-government and will retreat even further into their private worlds to insulate themselves and secure themselves against the troubles and deficits of the world around them.

In each of the communities profiled, citizen participation is an essential part of the local problem definition and policymaking process. Jacksonville, Hampton, Owensboro, and Wilmington have implemented civic dialogue in different ways, but all have benefited from it. Through a commitment to local democracy, these communities have been able to more effectively address problems such as teenage pregnancy, access to health care, and youth development. At the same time, they have fostered a civic culture that encourages and expects broad community collaboration in tackling a host of other challenges. Any community can profit in multiple ways from connecting citizens with local government, with community organizations, and with one another. Deliberation is a vehicle to get citizens back to the table, connect their interests and ideas, and actually solve problems.

Getting Started in Your Community

As demonstrated in this chapter, the process of civic dialogue can get its start in many places. The West Virginia Center for Civic Life joined with a local university and other partners to create forum guides on health care and public education, tailored to issues facing West Virginians. Several years ago, the *Charlotte Observer* launched a series called "Taking Back Our Neighborhoods" that stimulated talk and discussion throughout the community. Sometimes conversations begin in a public library. The point, of course, is to start where you are and with a group that is interested. Resources on ways to organize community forums on a multitude of issues are available from the National Issues Forums (www.nifi.org) or the Study Circles Resource Center (www.studycircles.org). For more ways to create opportunities for dialogue, see www.conversationcafe.org and www.jcci.org. There are ground rules so that discussions are not free-for-alls for people with a particular bone to pick. There are tips for people who are less comfortable facilitating or talking. There are organizations in the community that have public discussion in their mission, and there are multitudes of people who want to deliberate but also act. Find them and get a deliberative process going. It will make a difference.

Begin your search by contacting the National Issues Forums, Study Circles Resource Center, Conversation Café, your local League of Women Voters, and your local library. One or more of these sources should provide a contact in your community. If all else fails, start something yourself—in your home, with a religious organization, or as part of a study club.

6

Preserving the Past

Inspired by the Past, A Vision for the Future
Birmingham Civil Rights Institute

I t has been said that a city without old buildings is like a person
without a memory. Every community in America benefits from
sites, structures, places, and neighborhoods that provide links to its
past. Some communities have learned, however, that these historic
landmarks and landscapes can also provide a link to a community's
future.

Framing the Issues

The purpose of this chapter is to illustrate how communities can
use their past to positively affect their future. This is more than the
restoration of buildings; it is about a broader concept of *owning the
past* and using it to positively inform decisions. It is also about
including a wide array of interest groups, often with conflicting goals
and ideas, to cooperate and coalesce around the same vision.

The communities profiled have been very successful in placing
themselves in a context that builds on the past. In Charlottesville,
for example, planners and business owners wanted to "save" downtown, but they also wanted to "create" downtown anew. The Birmingham Civil Rights Institute created the vehicle to acknowledge

and honor a painful past but simultaneously built a resource that would educate the next generation on human rights. Lowell's historic mills provided the opportunity to re-create history as a pathway for education and pride in the community's past and future. Asheville's citizen movement to preserve downtown has proven to be a boon to preservation but also to the creation of a viable economic and civic community. Asheville "came back" by way of its history and culture. Denver's Lower Downtown is both an economic development and preservation success story. By preserving, the city allowed its "birthplace" to reclaim its place.

This chapter will sort out some nuts-and-bolts information about retrofitting and uses of buildings, but it will also discuss the reclaiming of history and culture to create a larger vision for the future.

Preservation Brings Both Aesthetic and Economic Advantage

It's widely accepted that civic beauty and pride in community heritage are benefits often associated with historic preservation, but more and more researchers are beginning to take note of the economic advantages of preservation.

Revitalization Campaigns

Among the best-known and most economically successful forms of historic preservation are downtown revitalization campaigns. For instance, the Main Street Program, established by the National Trust for Historic Preservation in 1980, demonstrates that downtown revitalization can be an important component of the economic renewal of cities, towns, and neighborhoods, as Boston has demonstrated. Existing infrastructure downtown means that communities need not build new streets or water and sewer lines and thus allow investments to be in buildings and amenities. Downtowns are often still the greatest employment sectors within cities, serve as incubators for new business, and are the focal points for businesses and residents in the city and in some instances the whole region (Tyler, 2000, p. 171). Not the least important, downtown revitalization may address growing concerns about suburban sprawl. Rypkema (1994) has pointed out that more intensive use of buildings and sites already in place may be one of the most effective methods of preventing sprawl.

Rather than giving up on older neighborhoods or downtowns, which some businesses and residents abandoned years ago, renewal efforts build on existing assets. Preservation efforts generally encourage communities to recognize that they have design options other than strip malls and high-rise office buildings, and older buildings can be more architecturally interesting.

Adaptive Use

Another economic development strategy for older buildings is called *adaptive use*. Apart from aesthetic and historical considerations, demolishing existing buildings and constructing new ones is a costly proposition vis-à-vis the labor, materials, and craftsmanship needed for new construction projects. Rehabilitation is often seen as an expensive option, but studies have found that rehabilitation costs per square foot are often significantly less than the costs of new construction (Tyler, 2000, p. 185).

The adaptive use approaches take advantage of existing structures that might otherwise be destroyed and transforms them for alternative uses. The federal government and at least twenty states encourage private investment in historic buildings by offering tax credits for rehabilitation, giving businesses an incentive to preserve rather than destroy (Michigan Historic Preservation Network). For example, in San Francisco's Ghirardelli Square, an old chocolate factory became an internationally famous shopping center. In Charlottesville, the downtown post office was transformed into the main branch of a regional library. In Boston, Faneuil Hall, once a government meeting place, is now a major tourist attraction with shops and eateries. Elsewhere, factories have been turned into convention centers, train stations have been transformed into restaurants, and department stores have been converted into hotels. Aside from its economic advantages, the adaptive-use approach benefits the environment: the National Trust for Historic Preservation dubs it "the ultimate recycling."

Increased Property Values and Increased Tourism

Historic preservation, downtown revitalization, and adaptive use benefit the entire community as well as particular segments, such as businesses, merchants, and home owners. Designating a particular neighborhood or district a historic place can enhance property values and resale opportunities for individual home owners. A report by the Michigan State Historic Preservation Office notes that "the stabilizing influence and protection that a historic district provides also may encourage private investment and increase property tax revenues for local governments" (Michigan Historic Preservation Network). In this way, the benefits that individual home owners reap from preservation may spill over and affect the community as a whole, leading to aesthetic improvements in historic districts as well as greater local tax revenues, according to the National Trust for Historic Preservation.

It is no secret that historic sites, structures, and landscapes are popular tourist attractions. Heritage tourism has become more popular since the early 1990s, as Americans seek to combine recreation with educational experiences that teach them about local and national history. A 2002 survey by the Travel Industry Association found that 81 percent of American adult travelers included at least one arts, heritage, or cultural activity on a trip; this translates into almost one hundred eighteen million travelers per year. In addition, research has found that vacationers who visit historic sites tend to stay longer and spend more money than other types of travelers (National Trust for Historic Preservation).

Links to Our Community and to Our Past

Saving and restoring older structures have a number of benefits other than purely economic. It does not take an architect or a designer to recognize that older structures are often more aesthetically pleasing than newer ones. The National Trust for Historic Preservation notes that some older buildings are "a gift to the street" because their style, texture, material, and charm—and perhaps even eccentricity— enrich and enliven their surroundings. Historic places contribute to a unique sense of community identity, character, and beauty that once demolished cannot be re-created.

Perhaps most important, historic sites, structures, and districts link a community to its past, promoting a sense of community consciousness and connectedness that high-rise office buildings and parking garages simply cannot. By protecting reminders of the past and safeguarding a community's heritage, preservation makes history available to future generations. Vibrant downtowns, lush landscapes, and historic structures tell a story that reminds a community of where it has been and maintains a sense of identity over time. One report warns that without historic preservation efforts, "History will be relegated to the occasional museum visit, and only acknowledged by those residents or visitors interested enough to seek it out. However, by engaging in serious preservation efforts, community leaders can ensure that the past has a constant presence and is not forgotten" (Price [see Web site]). History and tradition can be a region's greatest cultural and economic assets, and their unique character makes them irreplaceable.

Historic preservation is a smart investment vis-à-vis aesthetic beauty, economic development, and community identity. It can instill civic pride, generate tourism, revitalize downtowns, spur economic development, and educate citizens about their local heritage (Virginia Department of Historic Resources Web site). The attractiveness of a glitzy urban center or a "quaint" small town may seem less important when compared with challenges such as affordable housing or the quality of public education. Community leaders must weigh the different options for investments that can make a community strong and attractive; it's never a cut-and-dried decision. Fortunately, communities often do not need to choose between preservation and economic development. Preservation can provide economic as well as civic and cultural benefits for all kinds of communities. Buildings, museums, and historic districts help people learn. They are visible reminders of days and times gone by. They bind people in a shared, if not common, set of circumstances.

No More Just Knocking Down or Paving Over

One of the most interesting aspects of asking questions about communities is that you get unexpected answers. Invariably, in the research for this book, answers to revitalization questions turned to what was lost as well as what was saved. In a conversation about preservation, one local historian commented that citizens in her community still lament the loss of the "ridge." The mountain ridge framed this city until the early 1950s, when the desire to be the first city in the state to connect to the interstate highway system caused one end of the ridge to be destroyed and with it a beautiful residential and environmental area. Many people are still sorry and say so. For other communities, it is a movie theater, a train station, or a historic home. Citizens in San Antonio grimace when they think that their treasured Riverwalk had to be saved in 1926 from its designated fate as a paved-over storm sewer! Balancing progress and preservation has always been a challenge. Although the multiple parties in such decisions have different views on the wisdom of one direction over another, there are some basic points that citizens should know.

First, experience has taught that there should be enforced guidelines for the decision-making process for demolishing buildings of historical significance. In some cases, the buildings that should be saved are not on the historical register. Rather, they hold important cultural, social, *and* historical significance to the fabric of the community. The "ridge" was not a historical building, but it is sorely missed. Who has the last say and why? Second, there must be a waiting period. Communities must have enough cooling-off time so that decisions are not bulldozed (literally and figuratively) through the system. Why rush? Third, there should be a broad-based committee, including local government, business, citizens—from throughout the community—that considers the opportunity costs of losing buildings, green space, and even stands of trees. These are irreplaceable things that need attention and thought. Communities need a process of deciding about the fate of older structures as much or more than they need a process of deciding about new development.

People still want to remember the familiar and learn from it. The home of Thomas Jefferson, Monticello, is a pristine example of preservation extending history. Monticello is surely better maintained than it was in Jefferson's time. That house, like many others throughout the country, is much more than the home of a famous person. It is a research center, public history museum, and gateway to understanding the nineteenth century. The same can be said of many places in every state and community—preservation allows us to learn.

The One That Got Away

One decision in a city's history is the archetype of a range of missteps in decision making that provides a wake-up call for all communities. In 1909, Birmingham, Alabama, built one of the grandest train stations in the Southeast. The Terminal Station was a two-turret structure, featuring a dome sixty-four feet in diameter with a skylight. The station had a seventy-six-hundred-square-foot waiting room with Tennessee marble walls (Marye, 1909). It was a teeming place in the 1930s, 1940s, and 1950s. Its peak period saw fifty-four trains per day. According to Richard Pleaumons, a passenger agent for the Southern Railroad for almost forty years, the station's demise actually began in the late 1950s, with increased reliance on the automobile. "Some people blame the airlines," he said, "but it was cars that put the railroads out of the passenger business." By 1960, there were only twenty-six trains per day. Less than a decade later, there were only seven. Although freight still came through Birmingham, it was clear that the great age of passenger service was over (Kelly, 1998).

Interestingly enough, what appeared to be a boon to Birmingham and other urban areas was the premature death knell for the Terminal Station. In 1969, President Richard Nixon signed an executive order that mandated that all new federal office buildings be built in urban areas. The possibility became a reality when the Social Security Administration announced plans for a new service center in Birmingham. This possibility piqued the interest of a local developer, who approached the station's owner, the Southern Railroad, about retrofitting the site to accommodate not only the new Social Security complex but also other developments. The net effect was to jump-start downtown Birmingham's redevelopment to the tune of $10 million and three thousand jobs, but it required the demolition of the almost vacant Terminal Station. The negotiations were done privately for the most part; the mayor, the city council, and the public learned of it late in the game. During the time that the station could have been saved, there had been no real discussion of possible uses or how development could include the station.

The Heart of Dixie Railroad Society lobbied for it to become a transportation museum. Gilbert Douglas Jr., a member of the club, said, "Birmingham didn't have much by way of history to start with, and even though some people look upon the building as a monstrosity, it could be a major tourist attraction" (Richardson, 1969). Local architects joined in, calling for the preservation of the unique architectural character. The station had allegedly dodged a bullet in the early 1960s, when a new post office was eyed for the site but was sited several blocks away. The final death march began on June 30, 1969, when the Alabama Public Service Commission approved an application by the developer to go forward with the Social Security development. Objections by witnesses attempting to preserve the building as a historic landmark were overruled. At the hearing, Warner Floyd, executive director of the Alabama Historical Society said, "The proposed demolition of Terminal Station would involve 20 percent of the architectural heritage assets of a city of three-quarters of a million people." The commission, however, felt that its jurisdiction was limited to "the convenience and necessity of the traveling public." Assurances from the owner that the rights of railroad workers would be protected met those limits. The plan was approved for the Terminal Station to be razed and the property to be used for the six-story Social Security building and parking for twelve hundred at a cost of $10 million. Future plans included a "huge" motel and two more office buildings (Beiman, 1969).

Even though there was vocal opposition by members of the city council and the public, it just was not enough or in time. However, there was not a groundswell in any corner to stop it. The station was a dirty eyesore with an eclectic architectural style. The idea of jobs and development in a blighted area made sense to many as a fair trade-off. The Terminal Station was razed in 1969 and 1970.

There were grand politics played in this decision from many sides. There was money to be made in the development, an expressway that needed an alternate route, and an uncommitted public. The mayor at the time, George Seibels, lamented that it was an opportunity that was not just lost but never existed. "We just didn't have enough information to try to coordinate the various interests that would have had to come together to save it," according to Seibels (Kelly, 1998).

Lots of "might have beens" have been discussed in the last thirty-five years. Former mayor David Vann, who opposed the demolition of the terminal, cited a 1977 change in the federal tax law that provided grants, tax breaks, and other inducements to encourage preservation and restoration. Financially, that vehicle for preservation might have made a difference. Birmingham learned the lesson of preservation the hard way. The worst "might have been" of all was that the Social Security complex was never built on the site—in fact, nothing has been built on the site. Now more than three decades later, the most visible structure on the eleven acres on 26th Street North are concrete buttresses of an expressway. There are no buildings, hotels, or even parking lots.

Birmingham was certainly not alone in its decision making. According to Potter (1996, pp. 540–546), thousands of stations were demolished in the second half of the twentieth century. Portland, Maine; Atlanta, Georgia; Chicago, Illinois; and San Francisco, California, also lost their stations in the sixties. They were joined by priceless historical buildings and homes.

The reason Birmingham's experience has currency today is that we know that the preservation of history is important to a community's store of civic capital. Perhaps former mayor Seibels described the broader lesson best: "The great shame is that Birmingham lost one of its most glorious landmarks to an ill-conceived proposition. It's certainly the most unpopular razing of any structure in the city's history, and although it probably took another ten or fifteen years after we lost the Terminal Station, we now seem to put a great deal more thought into what a particular building or landmark means to the fabric of the community. There's no more just knocking things down" (Kelly, 1998, p. 17).

Cities that have realized the need to restore, rehabilitate, and reclaim their buildings and their history have generally had win-win results. History was saved and a future was created.

Saving What We Have

The communities profiled in this chapter have made some smart decisions about the landmarks and events of their past. Have all of their decisions been smart? Certainly not. However, the examples in this chapter illustrate the surefootedness that must exist for preservation, restoration, and a recognition of the past to happen. The critical ingredients are skill, patience, tenacity, vision, and determined leadership. Lowell, Massachusetts; Birmingham, Alabama; Charlottesville, Virginia; Asheville, North Carolina; and Denver, Colorado, have preserved their past as building blocks for the future. Citizens, local government, the federal government, and business played major roles in making the end goals a reality.

Lowell: The Spindle City

Lowell, Massachusetts, was the site that Massachusetts Governor Mitt Romney chose to kick off his 2002 gubernatorial campaign. In his remarks on July 12, 2002, he called Lowell a "model urban community" that should be an example to other cities across the country of how historic preservation and pride in a community's heritage can spur redevelopment. Long known as the Spindle City, the story of Lowell's rise and fall as an industrial city is really the story of the Industrial Revolution in the United States. For much of the nineteenth century—from 1826 until the 1890s—Lowell was among the largest and most impressive industrial cities in the world. Innovations in corporate structure and industrial technology kept Lowell at the forefront of the American industrial scene well into the 1900s. The flight of textile corporations to the South for cheaper, unorganized labor, beginning in the 1920s, dealt the communities of the Northeast and Midwest a blow from which some have still never recovered. By 1926, a rash of closings and relocations left only three of the original textile corporations operating in Lowell. The Depression hit Lowell hard, and total textile employment dropped from a high of twenty-two thousand in 1924 to eight thousand in 1936. Some mill complexes were torn down or allowed to slide into disrepair. World War II brought brisk demand for cloth, and the remaining mills did well during those years. Remington, General Electric, and U.S. Rubber competed with the Amers, Merrimack, and Boott textile companies for workers, so conditions improved and wages tripled. The year 1945 brought an economic downturn, however, as defense contract money dried up, and the Boott and Merrimack mills finally closed in the 1950s. Many mill boardinghouses were razed, as was the old tenement neighborhood of Little Canada. The empty century-old factories stood as looming and sometimes unwelcome reminders of the Lowell of the past. Young people were leaving, and those that stayed "were ambivalent about their history, recalling the hard conditions under which their parents had worked" (Lowell Historical Park Web site).

Civic leaders began to form a challenging new vision of Lowell in the early seventies. Educator Patrick Mogan, one of the key leaders, insisted that the revitalization be based on Lowell's industrial and ethnic heritage. Lowell's distinguished past, Mogan believed, could be used to reinvigorate the community, stimulate the economy, and improve the educational system. "Lowell had a low image of itself," according to Martha Mayo, head, Center for Lowell History. "Pat Mogan and others had the notion of using the city as a classroom to improve self-esteem." The Lowell Plan and the Lowell Development and Finance Corporation changed the course of Lowell's path from a community of decline to rebirth. A major component of the plan was the creation of a historical park, which would showcase the city as a living museum and provide a springboard for redevelopment. This group first enlisted the support of the local government, winning endorsement from the city council in 1972. The Lowell Heritage State Park emerged in 1974 from this cooperative effort. The effort did not stop there, however. Paul Tsongas, then Senator from Massachusetts, had grown up in Lowell and became a vocal advocate for making Lowell into a national park. Senator Edward Kennedy also supported the initiative. In 1978, after several years of study and hearings on the plan, Lowell National Historical Park was created along with the Lowell Preservation Commission. The Park Service was charged with stabilizing, cataloguing, and interpreting Lowell's past. The Preservation Commission faced a similar challenge: stabilizing and restoring the massive physical infrastructure of historical Lowell. As the park would be situated in the heart of downtown Lowell, it was clear that the larger mission of the Park Service presence in Lowell would be to restore and encourage private redevelopment of the city. "What occurred was not just redevelopment," remembers Mayo, "but really the coming together of four circles of action: the preservation community, the federal Model Cities program, the city planning office, and the congressional delegation." At the same time, educational opportunities in Lowell improved, with the University of Lowell's formation (now the University of Massachusetts-Lowell) from the merger of Lowell State College and Lowell Technological Institute in 1975 (Lowell Historical Park Web site).

Lowell had a dramatic transformation during the following decade. Overall a hundred old buildings were rehabilitated, including the Boott and Merrimack mills complexes and the old Bon Marché department store on the historic Merrimack Street in downtown. Wang Laboratories, a major international high-tech firm built a new facility and leased space in one of the major mill complexes for its hardware production and distribution facilities. The National Park Service located its Visitors Center in part of another mill complex and partnered with the city and a housing development corporation to rehabilitate the rest of the complex for residences and offices. At the Boott Cotton Mills complex, the Park Service took over about a third of the former mill for its museum and park offices. The University of Massachusetts-Lowell collaborated with the Park Service to run the Tsongas Industrial History Center, an educational, hands-on learning center for school groups, on several floors of the Boott Cotton Mills complex. The rest of the complex has been redeveloped as office and warehouse space and planned housing. One of the few remaining boardinghouses, once serving New England farm girls who came to work the looms between 1836 and the 1940s, became the Park Service's Boardinghouse Exhibit and was connected to the newly constructed Mogan Cultural Center, housing University of Massachusetts-Lowell's Center for Lowell History and serving as rehearsal and performance space for a number of cultural organizations.

The boom of the 1980s in Lowell softened with the rest of the national economy. Lowell has continued an upward path in terms of redevelopment, even with the departure of Wang Laboratories in 1992, laying off a substantial number of workers and depressing the local economy for a time. Yet the sense of pride in Lowell is unmistakable. Now Governor Mitt Romney's description of Lowell as a model urban community echoed Senator Paul Tsongas's words, spoken in Congress during the debate over the creation of the national park: "Twelve years ago, Lowell decided that its identity was important. Important to its people and the Nation. There are hundreds of people who should be credited for discovering this America. Many workers . . . wanted the good and the bad of the past preserved, rather than flattened and denied" (Tsongas [see Web site]).

The population has grown over the past two decades as new immigrants have replaced the traditional Irish, Greek, Portuguese, French Canadian, and other groups who had replaced the first Yankee mill girls in the 1840s. Now Southeast Asian, Latino, and West African groups make up an increasingly large part of the community. A local Cambodian association estimates that Cambodians currently make up about 25 percent of Lowell's 106,000 residents ("Lowell's Cambodian Community").

Renewed economic prosperity in the late 1990s brought hope again to the city. The dream of a revitalized community that was envisioned three decades ago has become, through careful planning and determined work, the hub of redevelopment throughout the city. According to Mayo, people are finding Lowell a very attractive community. Lowell has used its past to build its future.

Birmingham: Owning the Past

Birmingham, Alabama, was an industrial city that drew its strength, wealth, and resources first from its rich veins of iron ore and then from steel. Founded in the mid-nineteenth century, the Birmingham area grew, rapidly reaching a population of 400,000 by 1930. It had two nicknames: the "Magic City" because it grew from a small town to a big city almost overnight and the "Pittsburgh of the South" because of its steel-making prowess (Norrell, 1993, pp. 177–178). However, Birmingham's real notoriety came in the sixties when it became the focal point of the civil rights movement. White resistance to integration was fierce. The Reverend Fred Shuttlesworth, a local pastor and head of the Alabama Christian Movement for Human Rights, invited Martin Luther King Jr. and the Southern Christian Leadership Conference staff to assist in the

Birmingham movement. However, a Sunday morning in September 1963 changed Birmingham and the world forever. A bomb was placed in the Sixteenth Street Baptist Church, killing four young African American girls. The world mourned Birmingham Sunday. Birmingham was seen as the center of racism and segregation.

Political leaders led by former mayor David Vann and then mayor Richard Arrington sought to create a civil rights museum as a center for reconciliation in the late seventies. After a visit to the Holocaust Museum in Jerusalem, Vann proposed a resolution to the city council to establish a civil rights museum. The resolution passed unanimously in 1979. Vann, law clerk to Justice Black when the *Brown v. Board of Education* decision was handed down, remembered that the project "did not meet with instantaneous success" (Gates, 2002, p. 17). Part of the resistance was embarrassment and shame, but a part was also vestiges of the past. It was difficult to get white leaders to visibly identify with the museum. Naysayers said that such a place would open up old wounds, reinforce the negative impression about Birmingham, be a harborer of troublemakers, and last but not least, no whites would come to the museum, recalled Odessa Woolfolk, president emeritus of the Birmingham Civil Rights Institute. These prevailing sentiments made the launch of the project, to remember and learn from the past, rocky and tenuous. However, the supporters were inspired to do something positive about Birmingham's history. (This stands in stark contrast to Birmingham's colossal failure to remember its past, which was discussed in the Terminal Station example earlier in this chapter.)

It took seven more years for then mayor Richard Arrington, the first African American mayor since Reconstruction, to see the idea of a museum become a reality. A diverse task force was appointed, which included Vann and Woolfolk, director of Urban Affairs at the University of Alabama in Birmingham, as chair. The first step was to raise funds. A $65 million city bond issue was first proposed in 1986, with $10 million to go to the creation of the museum; it failed twice in two years. There was sentiment that given the depressed economy, Birmingham needed other things more. There was still a real concern that a visible reminder of the past would further damage Birmingham's image. Although the African American community supported the museum overall, there were some objections that there was a lack of representation of "foot soldiers" in the effort. Also, some people—white and African American—didn't see a need for a museum. But Arrington and others were not deterred (Gates, 2002, p. 20).

The final funding breakthrough came from the Historic Preservation Authority, which issued an $8 million bond, and from capital generated from a city land swap. A group of white and black businesspeople formed a task force to raise additional funds from the corporate community. Even after the money was raised, according to Woolfolk, the dissension continued. "Some people felt that the money could be used to fix potholes, fund public works projects, or improve the schools." The corporate community, in contrast, had come around. The fundraising campaign yielded $4.2 million—$1 million more than the goal. There was a sense that the museum was the right civic thing to do, says Woolfolk.

The institute opened in 1992 to a fanfare of visitors, local, national, and international. It was designed to tell the story of the past, but it was also to be a center for human rights for the present and the future. It has become a national and international center for reconciliation and human rights. Bishop Desmond Tutu has stated that it was the Birmingham struggle that inspired the people of South Africa.

The location of the institute is important. It sits across the street from the Sixteenth Street Baptist Church and Kelly Ingram Park. The church was a symbol of the movement. The park was the central gathering place in the sixties, where so many citizens and foot soldiers were arrested. The whole area surrounding the institute has been designated as the Civil Rights District.

The contents of the institute are real, not sugarcoated. They include the jail cell that once held Martin Luther King Jr., Fred

Shuttlesworth's Bible, a Ku Klux Klan robe, a copy of *Brown* v. *Board of Education* signed by all nine justices, school desks, papers, photos, even a bus of the same vintage as one ridden by the Freedom Riders.

The institute has helped Birmingham own the past. Thousands of people from over a hundred countries and of all races have visited the institute. A decade since its founding, Woolfolk says, "The Institute recognizes the redemptive importance of memory. It is both a time capsule and a modern-day think tank focused on seeking equitable solutions to common problems" (Birmingham Civil Rights Institute, 2002). The institute is a place not only to understand the history of the past but also to make it. A curriculum has been developed with an emphasis on human rights. Programs for school children help them understand the effects of racism and prejudice. It is a place to learn about the richness of the arts, culture, and heritage of Birmingham's African American community.

The Birmingham Civil Rights Institute is not just a museum or an educational institution: it's a major step forward for a community that must remember its past in order to re-create its future. With premier medical facilities, research centers, and higher education institutions, Birmingham is moving forward on many fronts. The institute is an important piece of the mosaic that includes Birmingham's past and future.

Asheville: The Jewel in the Mountains

Asheville, North Carolina, was cited by Richard Florida as the eleventh of 124 cities on his creativity index ranking of cities under 250,000 population (Florida, 2002). This designation only begins to reveal the creative economy that Asheville is generating in its modern-day renaissance. A city of almost 70,000, it is a city of contrasts: strong religious values and dedicated work ethic juxtaposed with free expression, inclusiveness, and a thriving downtown hub. Asheville has found its rhythm. However, it has not always been so good.

Asheville's modern development began around the turn of the twentieth century. It was the resort destination of grand hotels, health resorts, and spas. It had more than fifty boardinghouses, as depicted by Thomas Wolfe in *Look Homeward, Angel*. Asheville's population grew from about 4,000 in the late nineteenth century to more than 50,000 twenty-five years later. Clearly, it was a city on the move, with thousands of tourists and a growing year-round population (Ready, 1986, p. 78).

The city was bursting at the seams with real estate speculation, physical expansion, heavy borrowing, and a growing population in the twenties. About that time, the real estate market began to slide, and when the Great Depression hit in 1930, Asheville became one of its worst victims. At 9 A.M. on November 9, 1930, the city's four major banks closed. Unfortunately, Asheville's leadership had spent tremendous sums to improve the city's appearance in order to attract visitors and tourists. As early as 1922, tax revenues were declining, so the city issued and sold municipal bonds—more than $23 million worth. Asheville's debt in 1930 was higher than that of Raleigh, Durham, Winston-Salem, and Greensboro combined, and the city could not meet its obligations. Through a restructuring plan, the city did not go bankrupt, and future indebtedness was limited by severely constraining municipal spending. It took Asheville until 1976 to repay its Depression debt—forty-six years (Ready, 1986, p. 88).

During that almost half century, there were significant public works projects on the Blue Ridge Parkway, so Asheville fared better than many places. As Herbert Miles wrote in the *Asheville Citizen-Times*, "Have faith in yourself, . . . in Asheville, . . . and . . . have patience. Let us pay the piper for we have danced! And we shall dance again" (Ready, p. 92). They certainly tried, but times were very hard. In fact, the bitter memories of Asheville's quest to become "the Queen City of the mountains" scared and angered citizens—they had seen and heard too much. For more than forty years, political campaigns focused on preventing annexation, consolidation, or cooperation with the county. For all intents and purposes, the seventies saw Asheville at a standstill, except for the dollars invested by the Appalachian Regional Commission in the interstate highway system, the location of federal and state agencies in Asheville, and outside investments in urban development and health care. Theses changes began to lure locals back to the city. Ever present was a strong preservation effort, a thriving artistic community, and a wealth of beautiful architecture.

There was no urban renewal to speak of in the 1950s and 1960s. Many projects just could not get off the ground without public indebtedness. However, with the debt paid off, Asheville could finally look to the future. As early as 1977, the city council created the Asheville Revitalization Commission, charged with the physical, economic, and cultural development of the central business district. As the commission's report on the community reflected, "Asheville, the City in the Land of the Sky, can continue its slow, easy path of following the lead of other cities—doing some good things, some bad things, or just doing nothing—or it can strike out on its own path. Preserving and building a uniquely livable city will not necessarily be the easiest path" (Asheville Revitalization Commission, 1978, pp. 11–12).

This participatory revitalization process identified four key aspects of Asheville's future development: livability, history, uniqueness, and accessibility. The future was just beginning and it looked very good. Asheville had lots to build on in the downtown. In fact, downtown Asheville has the second-largest number of art deco buildings in the Southeast, following only Miami Beach.

The story of Asheville's restoration is one of citizen empowerment and old-fashioned tenacity. In 1980, the Asheville Revitalization Commission was ready to share the fruits of its hard labor with downtown businesses and the general public. With the help of an outside developer, the proposal was to level 11.5 acres of downtown for an indoor shopping mall. So as not to raise the ire of the historical preservationists, the proposal called for razing the buildings but keeping the facades. The promise was a revitalized downtown that would lure suburban shoppers and rid the area of deteriorating buildings. The plan might have been approved had it not been for about twenty-five citizens who organized themselves as Save Downtown Asheville and vowed to fight what they felt was the desecration of a beautiful and potentially viable downtown. As Wayne Caldwell, one of the leaders, said, "It was a loose coalition of downtown business owners and citizens that grew into the Committee of 1000." The group had varying reasons for the opposition, ranging from the preservation of self-owned businesses, to historical preservation, to just-a-bad-idea advocates. On the other side of the fence was the Fact Finding Committee for the Urban Complex, composed of most of the key business leaders, who saw the redevelopment plan as the only way to save downtown Asheville. The line in the sand was clearly drawn.

Despite loud objections by the Committee of 1000, endless discussions, and presentations at weekly city council meetings, a decision was made to hold a referendum to finance the project with local revenue bonds. The Committee of 1000 campaigned hard against the measure. The bond issue failed two to one. Ashevillians were saying not only no to the project but also no to any more borrowing for expansion. Too many remembered 1930.

After the vote, the mayor appointed a group to look at alternative downtown development. The result, although not linear or easy, was a move to revitalize Asheville, keeping its small-town atmosphere and historical buildings. It was an uphill battle. In 1991, 80 percent of downtown was either empty or substandard. There was little residential occupancy in the city. To help middle- and lower-income people find housing in the city, the council earmarked one cent of a four-cent tax increase toward the Housing Trust Fund. The fund provided low-interest loans to developers who wanted to build affordable housing. Since the decision to save downtown, more than 100 downtown buildings have been rehabilitated and developed with $200 million in private funds. There are 230 downtown businesses operating at capacity. Grove Arcade, originally built in 1929, has been restored and is two-thirds occupied with 52 businesses (Williams and Boyle, 2003, p. A5).

Asheville's future changed in 1981 because a group of citizens said no. Their persistence has paid off. Asheville is one of the creative and cultural centers of the South, with a preserved downtown that is the envy of most. It is bustling and thriving. A series of articles in January 2003 (Barrett, 2003; Williams and Boyle, 2003) in the *Asheville Citizen-Times* proclaimed downtown Asheville as "on the verge." But some people think it has gone beyond "the verge." Donovan Rypkema, a real estate and economic development consultant based in Washington, D.C., calls Asheville "one of the great success stories in America for a city that size" (Barrett, 2003, p. A14). There are some citizens sitting in cafés, running downtown businesses, and displaying their art in one of a hundred or more art galleries who might be saying, "We almost lost the opportunity." Asheville made a smart decision thanks to the efforts of a small group of citizens who refused to follow the pack. Interestingly enough, the series of articles in the *Citizen-Times* did not mention the opposition in the city—that's too bad. Even with the inevitable old wounds that still exist, it is important to understand how Asheville reclaimed its past.

Charlottesville: A World-Class City

In the eighties, downtown Charlottesville, Virginia, looked bleak. Anchor stores were moving to the suburban mall, and small businesses were closing their doors. In 1984, Charlottesville embarked on a downtown revitalization effort that can provide lessons for all communities interested in renewing the health and viability of their downtowns. Located in the foothills of the Blue Ridge Mountains in central Virginia, Charlottesville (population 45,000) is home to a number of historical sites that attract thousands of visitors every year, including Thomas Jefferson's Monticello, James Monroe's Ash Lawn-Highland, James Madison's Montpelier, and the grounds of the University of Virginia. These attractions notwithstanding, in the late 1960s Charlottesville found itself facing many of the same problems confronting cities throughout the country: rapid suburbanization and the accompanying erosion of the central commercial and residential urban core. Retail sales in the central business district and real property assessments were down, and one consultant plan recommended that 65 percent of downtown buildings be rehabilitated or replaced because they were deteriorated or obsolete. Early attempts at urban renewal and rounds of planning had come to naught (Lucy, 2002, p. 9).

The city refused to abandon its hope for downtown renewal. Alvin Clements, who chaired a commission that considered how to deal with the deterioration of downtown from 1971 to 1976, reveals the philosophy that guided Charlottesville leaders during this crossroads in the community's history: "We thought downtown renovation was necessary, because it was the heart. If it went bad, the rest of the city would go with it" (Lucy, p. 9). With a firm commitment to the idea of downtown revitalization, city government enthusiastically spearheaded the revitalization effort. Charlottesville officials pored over reports from national consultants and began to implement a series of policies and concepts suggested by the consultants. The reports called on Charlottesville to create a downtown that would be clean, safe, and auto free, in order to encourage people to use the space for work, leisure, and entertainment. Throughout the revitalization process, public and private partnerships and citizen engagement provided needed capital, creative energy, and commitment. Put simply, the common goal was to make downtown Charlottesville a place where people would want to be. After more than twenty-five years of thoughtful planning, investor support, and citizen participation, that goal has undeniably been achieved.

As soon as the city made a commitment to downtown revitalization, the work began. A new parking garage was built; office buildings, restaurants, and shops opened; and new downtown housing was constructed. Private investments poured into the downtown area, and gross business receipts rose dramatically. Preservation was a key element of the master plan submitted by the consulting firm Lawrence Halprin & Associates in 1974, which stated that "the quality of character, scale, and texture of the older structures in downtown was a unique possession well worth maintaining" (Lucy, p. 36).

Buildings that had been vacated were not abandoned but were preserved and transformed for alternative uses, including an elementary school that became an art center, a post office that was transformed into a library, and an auto repair shop that eventually became the headquarters of a local television station. After being blocked twice in the late 1970s, efforts to create a historic preservation district along the pedestrian mall were successful in 1984. Buildings were going to be protected.

Concern for historic preservation guided decisions about the construction and character of the downtown mall. A design scheme featuring a tight grid, small blocks, and narrow streets created a pedestrian-friendly environment and a fifteen-block auto-free zone—quite significant for a city of Charlottesville's size. A task force composed of city officials and downtown businesspeople gave design guidelines to downtown businesses that limited colors and materials to those thought compatible with the character of the buildings, helping to create an attractive and aesthetically pleasing setting. Not least important, the community itself valued preservation as a desirable approach to design and renewal. As one report put it, "Preservation and adaptive use are processes that can be encouraged with local ordinances and administrative procedures. But local culture and values probably contribute more to success" (Lucy, p. 38).

The most visible manifestation of downtown Charlottesville's philosophy of preservation was the construction of the pedestrian mall beginning in 1976. William Lucy, a professor of urban and environmental planning at the University of Virginia, found that the pedestrian mall was cited by each person interviewed as the most important component of Charlottesville's downtown revitalization. The tree-lined mall has a number of restaurants, bookstores, and cafés and is frequented by street musicians, vendors, and strolling families. The mall is anchored by a hotel and indoor ice skating rink on one end and an amphitheater on the other.

The success of Charlottesville's downtown revitalization would not have been possible without collaboration between the city and other groups, including private investors, businesses, nonprofit organizations, and citizens. The city's decision to take a leadership role in downtown revitalization, however, was a critical first step in encouraging other community members to come on board. Tackling the revitalization project with persistence and enthusiasm, city leadership gave private groups and citizens the confidence that downtown revitalization was a process that they would remain committed to for the long term. Alvin Clements pointed out that "getting city government to take a major role was very controversial. . . . Many thought downtown was a business problem, not a problem for government" (Lucy, p. 78). But it was precisely the role of government that jump-started the revitalization effort. Citizen participation, too, has been a Charlottesville tradition since revitalization efforts began in the early 1970s. Citizen involvement has taken many forms over the years, including citizens' commissions, public meetings and roundtable discussions, planning and design task forces, and public hearings.

The nature of Charlottesville's political and administrative leadership has facilitated the process of forging partnerships with investors, other governments, and the public. Just as local government was critical in stimulating investments in downtown, the continuity of city leadership further stimulated downtown development. In Charlottesville, the same city manager was in office from 1971, as the revitalization process was being conceived, until 1995. His deputy became manager in 1995 and continues as city manager. Planning support has also been stable: Satyendra Huja served as city planning director from 1971 to 1998, when he moved into a new role as director of strategic planning. According to Lucy, political, policy, and administrative continuity "maintained a context in which investor confidence and public satisfaction were sustained" (p. 39). Although not all communities experience this level of continuity in leadership, to the extent it exists, it can foster public and business confidence and encourage long-range planning.

Intergovernmental cooperation has also been present in Charlottesville's downtown revitalization project. Cooperation between Charlottesville and surrounding Albemarle County facilitated several major projects, including a county office building, regional library, museum, and theater restoration. By forging connections with private developers, other governments, and citizens, Charlottesville gave each of these groups a stake in the outcome of downtown revitalization and a reason to work for its success.

A final element in the success of downtown Charlottesville has been the timing of the city government's decisions. Because the revitalization project began before downtown department stores relocated in suburban shopping malls, the loss of those stores was anticipated and occurred after the transition to a new downtown had already begun. By the time the major anchor stores had departed for outlying areas in Albemarle County, the evolution of downtown to a center for entertainment, specialty shops, cultural experiences, business, and civic life was already under way. In this way, city leaders addressed a situation—the growing attraction of retailers to suburban shopping malls—before it *became* a problem in their city. Smart communities invest in the prevention of problems through planning, analysis, and foresight that can allow them to address challenges before they become full-blown crises. In Charlottesville, "The department store exodus did not lead to panic," one report concludes. "In a sense, it was an expected part of the plan" (Lucy, p. 35).

An outside evaluation documented increases in gross receipts from downtown businesses, real property assessments, real estate sales prices, and new construction. Property values in downtown Charlottesville rose 10 percent in 1999, compared with 6 percent citywide, and commercial vacancy rates on the pedestrian mall were as low as 1 percent in July 2001. Not only have businesses profited from their location on the downtown mall, but pedestrians flock to the area and feel safe there—96 percent of Charlottesville residents reported feeling safe on the mall in a 2000 survey. The average number of pedestrians on the mall ranged from eleven hundred at lunchtime on weekdays to sixteen hundred on Saturday evenings to a high of thirty-five hundred for weekly summer concerts. There are more people downtown after 5 P.M. than during the day (Lucy, pp. 14–15, 29).

Downtown Charlottesville remains a success today because the city, private investors, and the public made a commitment to preserving the area's historical assets. They call themselves a world-class city, and they are certainly on the right track. Downtown has experienced several new investments in recent years that have built on the strong foundation already in place. The community has sought to promote the continued viability and attractiveness of downtown. Issues still remain such as affordable housing and consumer-goods shopping to name a few. As former city councilor David Toscano cautiously put it, "Downtown is a success, but it is fragile. It requires constant attention and reinvestment" (Lucy, p. 83).

The process of downtown revitalization in Charlottesville began with city leaders who made a vibrant new downtown area a priority. Those leaders developed a long-term vision, forged partnerships with outside consultants, property owners, and entrepreneurs, and solicited public input. The principles of historic preservation and pedestrian improvements guided the downtown revitalization process. The fact that the city took the first step gave businesses and citizens confidence that their collective persistence, leadership, and vision would one day come to fruition. Community leaders did not expect Charlottesville's downtown renaissance to take place overnight. Having set realistic goals and implemented plans to achieve them, community members were able to watch the revitalization of downtown Charlottesville unfold over many years—and they were rewarded for their patience.

Denver: The Gold Mine Neighborhood

Denver, Colorado, has always had a prominent place in the American West. Long considered the financial, manufacturing, agricultural, and cultural hub from Kansas City west, it has developed a diverse economy that includes financial services, oil and gas, media, tourism, major sports, and high tech.

In the 1980s, the recession hit the Denver area hard—very hard. According to former mayor Federico Pena, it was the worst recession that the city and state had ever experienced. The bottom fell out of oil and gas prices, real estate values plummeted, and businesses and banks failed. By 1988, fourteen thousand energy-related jobs had been lost, 50 percent of the total energy workforce. The downtown office vacancy rate was at 31 percent, and people were looking for answers (*Boundary Crossers*, 1997, pp. 78–80).

That answer came as Pena and others looked at the assets of the city and how they could be leveraged to stabilize and grow the economy. One obvious direction to look was: location, natural beauty, tourism, and development opportunities in Lower Downtown and the Central Platte Valley.

During this same time period, a group of eight people were thinking independently about the possibilities of and the need to protect Lower Downtown, the historic area of the city where Denver was born. This group of eight realized that Lower Downtown was a "gold mine as a neighborhood and the birthplace of Denver," says Lisa Purdy, at that time on the staff of Historic Denver. It was not just selected buildings that were important but the whole collection. In the early eighties, Lower Downtown was an aggregate of a few restaurants, low-rent hotels, and panhandlers. Buildings were beginning to be razed for parking lots to provide revenue for property owners. Renewed interest in the area occurred with a proposed plan to link the new convention center to the anchor building in the area, Union Station. Preservationists feared that putting a new convention center in Lower Downtown would cause destruction of Denver's birthplace and the historic buildings.

The saving, restoration, and development of Lower Downtown Denver is a sterling example of mayoral leadership, civic participation, and vision, but it was not easy or quick. It took almost six years.

The small breakfast group of eight, which included preservationists, Lower Downtown business owners, and developers, ham-
mered out a plan that included support for putting the convention
center behind Union Station in exchange for stronger controls on
demolition of historic buildings. Upon presentation to the executive director of the Denver Partnership (a downtown Denver
booster group), he promptly said that this would never work, that
the group was too small to make such a controversial plan acceptable to a larger constituency. As Lisa Purdy, one of the principals,
remembers, "I was really upset to hear this after all our hard work—
but he was right." He suggested that Purdy join a new task force
being convened by Mayor Pena. She was appointed as the "representative of the preservationists" to the new Downtown Area Committee. The twenty-eight-person committee was charged with
developing a comprehensive plan for all of downtown—one part of
which was Lower Downtown.

Earlier in 1982, the city had provided incentives for Lower
Downtown residential development with new zoning laws. However, a key piece was missing—demolition control—that is, who
had the final say on which buildings went or stayed. That issue came
to define the broader conversation as the process went forward
(Collins, Waters, and Dotson, 1991, pp. 74–76).

The mayor's Downtown Area Plan Committee completed its
work in May 1986. The final plan included a comprehensive package of recommendations for Lower Downtown as well as other parts
of downtown. It is important to note that it had been three years
since the group of eight held their weekly breakfast meetings. As
Purdy so aptly observed, "Tenacity is a very big element" in creating a vision and community change.

The plan called for creating distinctive districts throughout
downtown Denver. Lower Downtown was one of those designated
for both preservation and reinvestment. However, it took another
two and a half years before historic-district designation was adopted
by the city council. Having a plan with recommendations was a far
cry from an actual ordinance that put restrictions into legal form.

Hundreds of meetings took place, with property owners and preservationists looking for common ground. In 1988, the historic-district ordinance was finally passed and with it design standards on new construction, strict controls on the demolition of buildings, and a package of incentives for marketing plans for the area.

Property owners and developers opposed the designation, but Mayor Pena's leadership throughout the planning process proved essential, and at this point pivotal. The mayor had been supportive of the Lower Downtown development since the conversation began. As he says, "[We felt that we] ought to combine history with growth. The old and new were part of our unique assets." However, as he and others remember, property owners and developers argued that the restrictions on design, use, and demolition infringed on their ownership rights and would limit their ability to make a profit. Pena countered this with assurances that the city not only would provide economic enhancements to the district but also would step up infrastructure investment and law enforcement presence, as well as create a loan fund and make streetscape improvements.

The development of Lower Downtown was not smooth sailing. Opposition came from many sides, and even the preservationists disagreed at times. But the stalwart held firm. It was clear from other cities' experiences that there were some nonnegotiables in the process—a key one being demolition control. The mayor never wavered on this. The partnerships that were built throughout the process have stood the test of time. The collaborative nature of the Downtown Area Plan Committee brought divergent and convergent ideas together in new ways. According to former mayor Pena, "Nothing works without partnerships."

The story of Lower Downtown has evolved since 1988. The city followed through on its commitments and investments. A major league baseball stadium was built in the area with public-private funds, community development block grant money was provided for Lower Downtown loft housing, and property owners began to reinvest in the area. Even the chamber of commerce moved to Lower Downtown. In a report by Hammer, Siler, George

Associates (1990), the authors said this of Lower Downtown: "The research and analysis suggest that virtually all of the change to date has been positive and will likely accelerate in coming years." A 2003 article in the *Rocky Mountain News* reported that the office vacancy rate in Lower Downtown in these stark economic times is 12.7 percent versus the upper end of downtown, which is 20.74 percent. According to Doug Wulf, a local real estate officer, there is less square footage in Lower Downtown, but that is only part of the logic of the significant difference in occupancy rates. He cites the "twenty-four-hour" characteristic of downtown, which is shored up by downtown residential living and the recreational and entertainment options in Lower Downtown (Rebchook, 2003).

Denver is a model of building a broad constituency for development, redevelopment, and preservation. By capitalizing on the success of preservation, Denver is at the forefront of the national movement to integrate historical and cultural resources with tourism and convention industry. It is estimated that heritage tourism pumps millions of dollars into the local economy every year from multiple sources (Ditmer, 2001). These impressive results came after two decades of critical work and partnerships by all sectors.

Smart decisions need the input and thinking of many people from throughout the community. According to Pena, things work when the broader community embraces ideas and when it believes that positive change can happen. Second, smart decisions sometimes take time, are incredibly frustrating, and require incredible persuasion—because in the end, you can never be absolutely certain of an outcome. "There is no perfect knowledge," says Pena. What communities do have, as evidenced by Denver, are untapped assets, incredible energy, leadership at all levels, and a vision to make things happen—for which there is no substitute. One of the original breakfast group of eight, Lisa Purdy, says that the results of the hard work "are very gratifying," as she visits the area. The process was like "swimming up hill," but they made it by working together.

Lessons Learned: Sharing a Past and a Future

Downtown revitalization and preservation are not one-size-fits-all, and they don't often lend themselves to textbook analysis. Rather, says M. J. Brodie, president of the Baltimore Development Corporation, "Questions of urban development challenge traditional methods of planning and implementation, requiring new, sometimes radical—meaning 'from the root'—ideas, combining seemingly opposite or unrelated concepts into new paradigms, into synthesis of thought and action" (Brodie, 1997). Seven principles flow from this observation:

1. There must be an understandable physical vision—large enough to excite the imagination of all the participants, but structured enough that it can be achieved in the increments that realities of time and funding usually dictate.

2. The vision must be grounded in the authentic character of the place (its history, climate, terrain, cultural values) and informed by an articulated set of goals for the future— goals that describe what the city wants to be.

3. To implement the vision (the plan), a partnership must be formed between the public and private sectors, each sector bringing its skills to the process, to produce a better result than either could have achieved alone.

4. The public sector, through redeveloping the city's infrastructure (transportation, utilities, public open spaces), must set the stage for private investment.

5. A high level of quality must be set for design and construction (major redevelopment is often a once-in-a-generation opportunity!), in both public and private projects.

6. Methods must be developed to broaden the base of the redevelopment project, and to obtain not only cooperation but also enthusiasm from those involved.

7. A structure for implementation must be created that com-
bines responsibility with necessary authority, that is results
oriented and accountable to the citizens, and that is capable
of guiding the process over an extended period of time
(Brodie, 1997).

Downtown revitalization and historic preservation are never an
easy sell, but they can be done. Often the hardest step is the first
one. In these cases, communities of different sizes and situations
illustrate how Main Street or a museum or a historical district can
be the key to a new community development strategy. In very different venues and under widely divergent circumstances, these cities
all made decisions that built on values, history, and location. In
each case, the revitalization itself was a secondary result of the larger
accomplishment of citizen reinvestment—in one another and in
the place where they live.

These five illustrations weave a powerful story of partnership, citizen action, imagination, and honesty. Maybe that's what historic
preservation really is at its core. In each case, the motivation for
restoration went beyond economic development. The goal and the
outcome were bigger than that. The key to these examples is that
there was a vision of something beyond the buildings themselves. It
had to do with learning but also with remembering and respecting.

Getting Started in Your Community

What can your community learn from these illustrations? The first
thing is to recognize the importance of certain places, buildings, and
areas to the people who live there. Where are the familiar local
places that stir fond memories? As mentioned earlier, it can be a theater, a prominent home, or a place of worship. Second, it is equally
important to think imaginatively about a modern use. In Asheville,
one of its distinguished department stores is now a downtown hotel.

In Lowell, former textile mills are museums. Each of these communities found a broad range of stakeholders who wanted to preserve, honor, and build on the past; only part of the group were historic preservationists. The larger group included local government, business, educators, home owners, and citizens whose interests in the projects were far ranging. Preserving your community may begin with one question, "Who else might care?" Third, don't think it can't be done. Fourth, find out what kind of funding incentives might be available for the kind of restoration you have in mind. State historical or preservation associations are good places to begin your search. Contact the National Trust for Historic Preservation for ideas. Finally, keep in mind that all of the people in your community have a history and places that are special to them, even sacred. Remembering this helps build community through recognition and respect, which will build new relationships and trust.

7

Growing Leaders

We have to have a leadership that understands that its role is to create an environment for people to come together to attack the problems that confront them.

John Jacob

Building *bench strength* is a concept that coaches of team sports understand perfectly. Even though the most gifted players may start the game, there are others who are prepared and ready to play at a moment's notice. Building bench strength in civic leadership is the most critical challenge facing our communities.

The leadership called for today is found within a multitude of places and people. No longer is it necessary to think in terms of one leader or one group; American communities are filled with people who want to make a difference where they live.

As we think about the challenges facing the nation in its third century, none is more compelling than the need for more people to assume responsibility for leadership at all levels. For a community to achieve success, leadership must come from backyards and boardrooms.

Framing the Issues

This chapter will illustrate that leadership comes from all sectors and from all people. The notion that leaders must be elected, appointed, or anointed is no longer desirable or even possible. Communities need leaders who come through the ranks *and* the rank and file. None of this happens by serendipity or by wishing it were so. Leadership occurs when individuals step up to the plate on important issues and when there is a place for them to be heard.

The goal of this chapter is to identify the critical sources of leadership in communities—political, education, business, and civic—by providing examples of the collective difference it can make. Charleston has had the benefit of stable, progressive political leadership for a quarter of a century. The climate that the mayor and citizens have created together has borne fruit for the city. Higher education's role in change has been powerful over the years. No time has been more profound than in the development of Research Triangle Park in North Carolina. The collaboration formed by three academic institutions, state government, and businesses has created a lasting legacy to the force that higher education can be. Likewise, in Tupelo, business leadership was key to creating a different economic and social pathway to the future. Finally, citizens in Colquitt, Georgia, have proven that a few citizens can spark innovative collective action. The production of *Swamp Gravy* for ten years has allowed many voices to be heard. Leadership matters more than ever.

Many years ago, I witnessed a community situation that enlightened my view of civic leadership as few things have. A large project in an inner-city neighborhood had lost its original leaders. The project fell to a corporate group who had little knowledge or personal investment in the project. As the project failed to move forward as quickly as it should have, I suggested that some of the neighborhood leaders be included in the planning and implementation process. The response was, "There are no leaders in that neighborhood." There were people throughout the community who were ready to participate, solve problems, and, yes, lead, but the established leaders thought otherwise. Their impoverished view of leadership prevented the talents of far too many people from being fully used. We need leadership all right, but we must look broader and deeper to find the people we need.

A New Way to Think About Leadership

Three major shifts in the nation have affected how we must think about leadership. First, demographic diversity is increasing. Second, local decision making is more prevalent. Third, issues are more complex and interrelated. These shifts require that leaders know new things. The first shift requires that leaders have a cultural framework. The formal and informal leadership cadres in business, nonprofit organizations, government, and communities-at-large are becoming more reflective of the country as a whole. This requires an understanding of cultural differences in authority, communication, and public participation traditions. Further, leaders must be keenly aware of the barriers that have prevented participation among minority groups.

The second shift, local decision making, manifests itself in different ways. People want more control over the decisions affecting their lives. Further, citizens want more opportunities to interact with others on issues that matter. This requires that people have the skills to work more effectively with others through partnerships, collaborations, and deliberative processes.

Third, one agency or one sector cannot address the systemic problems in our communities alone. Issues cannot be siloed; they must be addressed multilaterally. Leaders must know how to identify community assets, how to manage conflict, how to communicate a broader agenda, and, finally, how groups can work together.

Leadership must no longer be thought of solely in singular terms. This is not to say that we should abandon personal reflection, self-knowledge, or individual skill improvement. Rather, this is a call for the civic side of leadership development. As we say at the Pew

Partnership, "It's about the 'we' not the 'me.'" We need more citizens to be at work in their communities than we ever have before. An expanded notion of civic leadership, however, will not happen on its own. This concept must be translated into the skills that are needed and applicable to both organizational and community life, and we must identify vehicles for delivering them. Although the lament for more leadership tends to focus on the national public arena, our greatest need may be for broader and deeper leadership capacity in America's communities.

As they think about the future, people in communities must ask these critical questions about leadership: What do we have? What do we need? and How we are going to get what we need? The topic of leadership has become a field of academic inquiry and the practice of training organizations locally, nationally, and internationally. There are national organizations connecting local chapters and convening people across the country. However, with all this important work on the study and practice of leadership, the critical and unsolved question is this: How can we spread it? The development of leaders has occurred in a relatively small percentage of Americans. Too few people have the access or the opportunity to actually learn the skills and build the relationships needed to be effective leaders in their communities. It is time to find and prepare our bench strength.

Finding New Leaders

The general consensus about leadership among most Americans is that we cannot have enough of it. The opportunities and challenges of the twenty-first-century world require the best and the brightest at the helm. This sentiment is probably right; more is better.

Leadership Is Critical Now

There are critical points where leadership matters most. It is those times that philosopher Hannah Arendt referred to in *Men in Dark Times* (1968), when she said that citizens have a right to perspective and action even in times of stress and distress. "We have the right to expect some illumination, and such illumination may well come less from theories and concepts than from the uncertain, flickering, and often weak light that some men and women, in their lives and their works, will kindle under almost all circumstances and shed over the time span that was given them on earth" (p. 1). This illumination comes from the expected as well as the unexpected places. Long-term progress will not happen unless there is a sense of ownership and responsibility for the future of the community that touches more than just the usual cast of players. We need illumination and leadership every day.

One of the reasons we turn to traditional leaders is that they are there. In the wonderful closing scene in *Casablanca*, when Rick, played by Humphrey Bogart, has killed the Nazi commander, his chief of police friend orders his men "to round up the usual suspects" for interrogation and then the two men walk away together. The "usual suspects" in our community lives are critical to solving important community dilemmas, but we cannot rely on them completely no matter their talent.

The "usual suspects" differ from community to community, but they are likely to include certain key businesspeople, well-known clergy, civic organization leaders, and representatives from local hospitals, schools, and nonprofit agencies. We need all those people in addition to shop foremen, postal workers, police officers, stay-at-home parents, young people, senior citizens, and public housing residents, to name only a few. We have to look broader and deeper. But how and where?

In his work on paradigm shifts, Thomas Kuhn (1996) found that it was actually young scientists who made many of the most significant discoveries. Applying this principle to community change suggests that involving young leaders with fresh ideas, enthusiasm, and new expertise can be greatly beneficial. The reality of today's challenges is that we can ill afford to exclude anyone's ideas from the community process. We have built too much of our lives and ways of working on the fault lines that divide us rather than on the ties that bind us. When the *work* is the focus in a community, not the personalities, vision supersedes individuals and ideas undercut stereotypes.

Potential Leaders Are All Around Us

In a partnership in the mid-nineties with ten midsized cities, I learned a tremendous amount about whom to look for and where. The project was called the Pew Civic Entrepreneur Initiative. Its purpose was to broaden the ranks of civic leadership from Anchorage to Jersey City. Community-based organizations had the responsibility of identifying sixty people over three years to participate in a national and local leadership program. The local partners found scores of people in their communities with untapped energy and interest. They ranged from postal workers to small-business owners to retired people. They had advanced degrees and no degrees. They represented over forty ethnic groups. In other words, it became absolutely clear that thousands of people in our communities need to be asked and need to be prepared to shed illumination on old problems.

The Promise of Leadership

Communities cannot build a beautiful environment or create an optimum climate, but they *can* cultivate people to enhance the prospects of the community and build a collective future. The illumination that Arendt describes is what happens when one person or a group of people can see through the fog of negative behavior, slim economic prospects, or compounded challenges to a way out and up. These leaders have vision and persistence. They "see it" and "see it through" (Thorpe, 1998).

Strong broad-based leadership is essential to community success. This leadership will change periodically, and the names of the people will surely change. That is the key to bench strength. Communities that rely on one industry, one family, or one perspective have missed the ideas, the resources, and the involvement of the "many." As communities consider their prospects for the future and who will carry the weight, they cannot look for one leader, *the* leader. Every community needs people "in the field," so to speak—backups and replacements with new skills—to create a winning community team. In baseball, you cannot just field a team of nine players. They get sick; they drop out; they move away. You must have reinforcements, trained and ready to play. As Yogi Berra would say, "You can observe a lot by watching" (1998, p. 95). If you watch successful communities, you'll see that they have strong leadership at all levels.

Success builds over time. Sure a big employer might be landed or a bond issue approved, but success over the long haul requires sustained effort, organization of the work, and collective vision and action. These occur most often because of *catalytic leadership*—people who can create the environment for working together toward common problems.

Luke (1998) suggests that the traditional "take-charge" leader is not successful in addressing complex community issues. What is needed are people who can convene multiple stakeholders, facilitate and mediate consensus around tough issues, and think and act strategically. These leaders must have a passion for change but flexibility on how to get there.

The notion that one person or a small group can "order" change is way off the mark. The people most affected by the problem, those that may have the most to gain or lose, must be part of the leadership and decision making in a community. Exclusion has never worked, and it never will. As Alice Day, assistant director of the Texas Drug Enforcement Commission explains, "More people are convinced now that we have to figure out in our own community what is best. . . . We need expert guidance on what the research shows . . . but there is no change until people change" (Pew Partnership for Civic Change, 1998, p. 67). People change when they are included and talked with, not talked at, and when they feel that they have something to contribute.

Leadership Matters Every Day

Strong leaders are important every day on Main Street or Wall Street. It is essential that communities expect the best and prepare for the worst as they do their day-to-day work. Leaders help set the course for communities. They look at the big picture. They act on the situation at hand. Crisis situations force citizens and communities to act. Often the decision-making options are limited by what must be done. Leaders who respond well to disasters are important to have. However, it is just as critical to have people who can anticipate problems and opportunities and put systems in place to minimize disruption, cost, or impact. In other words, would it be better to have a person who anticipates or one who responds? Obviously, we need both, but in all too many cases, leadership is just about responding. We need leaders who understand investing in community, working together, building on assets, creating community deliberation, building on the past, and expanding civic leadership.

Malcolm Gladwell's (2000) theory of the *tipping point* is a wonderful illustration of what effective collaborative leaders do: they tip the scales. The tipping point is the threshold at which ideas, trends, fashions, or even restaurants take hold. Leaders "tip" communities too. They can be the catalyst that pushes ideas and progress forward—or backward. Rarely do things just stay the same.

This notion of the tipping point—when diseases become epidemics or when a trend gets hot—helps us understand why the concentration of a broad and deep leadership team can make all the difference. The concentration of leaders in a community builds networks and relationships among citizens and organizations that are critical to make things happen. Who are those leaders we need and where do we find them? A group of highly successful nonprofit, government, and civic leaders describe these characteristics of good leaders: "saw the vision early on," "the glue that pulled it all together," "was more of an evangelist than an administrator," "very bright and very capable and very dedicated," "people with fire in their bellies." According to this group, they are traditional leaders, such as officeholders, business executives, and community foundation presidents, but they are also community leaders, such as neighborhood association members, knowledgeholders, and trusted neighbors (Harwood Group, 1998, p. 27). What can a broad-based group like this bring to the community table? Lots.

The leadership we need for communities is illustrated by the following cases. They represent political leadership, business leadership, educational leadership, and citizen leadership. There are many other groups who contribute to the leadership spectrum in a community—nonprofit organizations, labor, youth, seniors, religious organizations; the list goes on. As discussed in previous chapters, leaders at Abyssinian Baptist Church have both anchored and launched their community to new possibilities; citizens in small towns from Almena to Chimney Rock have created a dialogue about who they are and what is valuable; and in the case of Jacksonville Community Council Inc., a broad-based group of leaders has been convening for more than a quarter of a century to address tough community problems. And neighborhood leaders in Fremont are connecting across the community. Leadership can make a huge difference.

Leadership is an essential topic of conversation, but it also must be part of a strategic investment strategy. The case illustrations in this chapter demonstrate that leadership matters and matters a lot. Leaders from all sectors and places started what needed to be started, stopped what needed to be stopped, and imagined what had been unimaginable before.

Charleston: Elected Leaders Can Change the Future

A city like Charleston, South Carolina, is a perfect example of a leadership tipping point. Mayor Joseph Riley has been in office for a quarter of a century. For some communities, that kind of legacy might suggest a dynasty or the status quo. In Charleston, it suggests continuity in the midst of change and progress. When Riley took office in 1975, the city of Charleston was 16.7 square miles; today it is 90 square miles through annexation. Twenty years ago, the city was struggling with its downtown, balancing a military economy with a private one, and trying to create one community from a history of racial separation. Today it is a thriving example of what creative leadership can accomplish.

Perhaps Mayor Riley's greatest legacy will be his commitment to racial harmony and social progress. After his election in 1975, he worked aggressively to get more African Americans into leadership positions in the city and in the community. According to Bernie Mazyck, president and CEO of the South Carolina Community Development Corporation Association, the election of Joseph Riley as mayor was a major decision that has affected Charleston. "He brought a sense of fairness and justice to the community and made it clear that Charleston will only succeed if all the citizens have a chance to participate in the process."

The turning points for communities often center on events, values, or opportunities. In the case of Charleston, Riley's leadership has led them to address three:

1. Commitment to affirmatively and aggressively opening the government to everybody. (The practical application of this was to address racial challenges immediately and establish councils in neighborhoods throughout the city so government could listen better to citizens.)
2. Commitment to historic preservation.
3. Commitment to strategic planning and its follow-through.

Each of these strategies has been critical to Riley's leadership over the last quarter of a century. Racial harmony and progress were addressed head-on by the mayor in his first term and ever since. He brought the first African Americans into city government as department heads and hired Chief Reuben Greenberg, an African American, to head the police department. Further, Riley knew that city government had to do a better job of listening to citizens of all races but particularly those historically left out of the system. He established neighborhood councils across the city as vehicles for listening better. There are seventy very active neighborhood associations as a result.

Historic preservation defines Charleston on first glance. Riley's innovative approach to preservation has saved untold priceless structures and created a downtown restored as "the heart of the city." Using public-private partnerships as vehicles, Riley's efforts have pumped new life into areas throughout the city, with affordable housing, downtown development, and new amenities, like a minor league baseball stadium and an aquarium. Under the mayor's watchful eye, the old has not been replaced by the new but rather complemented by it.

Success in Charleston did not just happen. Rather than following every idea or notion, Charleston's leadership actually thought about what needed to be done. They did their homework and stayed the course. Amid the ruins of a devastating hurricane, an economic downtown, and the loss of the naval base, Riley encouraged, prodded, and led the community to pursue strategies that made sense for Charleston. The economy is now stable and growing, the arts community is thriving, home to the world-famous Spoleto Festival, and the civic capital investments are visible and bringing thousands of tourists and residents every day. Is Charleston where it wants to be? Probably it is not "there" yet. As Mazyck says, there is an unfinished agenda in the city for African Americans in particular. Although job creation in the tourist industry has boosted the economy and the job rates, it is not strengthening the ability of people at the lower end of the spectrum to build assets and financial wealth that secures families and thus builds the social and civic fabric of the community. Mayor Riley would likely agree. As he says, "If we are to build a great city and enhance the quality of life for every citizen, then we must realize that a great city is not great because of the size of its population. A city is great when it demands of itself excellence, protects its natural and built environment, and seeks a higher quality of life for every one of its citizens."

Leadership has mattered every day in Charleston, South Carolina. *Washington Post* columnist David S. Broder said, "What has been achieved here under his leadership has been truly extraordinary. . . . The way that Charleston treats the social problems that all old cities share has made Riley's long reign so remarkable" (Broder, quoted on City of Charleston Web site). Leadership focused on issues that can guide a community, economic prosperity, and equity creates new possibilities for communities of all sizes.

Mayor Riley has raised the bar on what mayoral leadership can do. Even in the current climate of partisanship and division, we can take heart that there are still real leaders in local government. For decades, that has often been where the civic-leadership conversation centered—elected leadership. Experience has taught us that elected officials need strong civic leadership from many corners and from many perspectives to do their jobs effectively. Communities that have been able to cultivate strong leadership layers have profited over time. Even dynamic and committed elected officials cannot make progress by themselves.

Tupelo: A Champion with a Newspaper

Tupelo, Mississippi, is a community that leads by example. Local newspaper owner, George McLean, epitomized that example. Located in the northeast corner of Mississippi, away from the Delta region, away from the state's capital in Jackson, in fact away from most anything, Tupelo is a hundred miles from Birmingham and Memphis. A city of 35,000, Tupelo is far from isolated. It is home to more than forty *Fortune* 500 or internationally recognized companies. The region, including Lee County, is the largest producer of upholstered furniture and the second-largest manufacturer of all furniture sold in the world. It has the largest nonmetropolitan health care facility in the United States (Tupelo Web site).

Tupelo's renaissance story began in the thirties with two important milestones. The city and surrounding areas were poor. Grisham describes it as "one of the poorest counties in the poorest state in the nation" (1999, p. 2). It had no natural resources, no advantageous location, and no real industry. In 1933, President Franklin Roosevelt himself brought some good news, making Tupelo the first city in the United States to be a Tennessee Valley Authority (TVA) community. The newly minted agency was charged with bringing not only electrical power to rural areas but also economic development efforts. Tupelo was a prime candidate for both. The second major development was the return in 1934 of Mississippi native George McLean. Born in Winona, Mississippi, south of Tupelo, but away for several years in graduate school and teaching, McLean arrived in Tupelo as the new owner of the then *Tupelo Journal*.

Beginning to breathe new life into a depression-hit community, McLean set about to become part of the civic leadership while raising the tough issues through the forum that the paper provided, issues ranging from labor relations to race. Things were beginning to gel for the community; prosperity was visible. In April 1936, McLean wrote an editorial entitled "It Can Be Done!" Two days later, a devastating tornado hit the area. When the paper reopened and McLean had pen in hand again, his inaugural editorial was "Tupelo Will Build on This Wreckage a Better and Greater City" (Grisham, 1999, p. 87). And they certainly have.

The Tupelo story has many interrelated and fast-moving parts. McLean and supporters were on a mission to improve the economic conditions of the community and thus the lives of the people. They understood and promoted three important principles of renewal: working together, education, and community involvement. All three ideas point to the same concept: we are all in it together. According to local leader and businessperson Jack Reed Sr., it was not always smooth sailing. McLean's views were considered more liberal than the views of a significant number of people in Mississippi—so much in fact that there was a move to get a competing newspaper to come to Tupelo. Reed said that McLean quieted his critics. George McLean was bright and intelligent, and he also got things done. He "put his money where his mouth was," says Reed. He gained people's respect, if not always their full endorsement.

In order for progress to gain a footing, McLean knew that there had to be local people and organizations to spearhead the efforts. The first of these structures was the Northeast Mississippi Poultry Council, established in 1936 to shore up the efforts of poultry farmers in the region through marketing and development. Although this initial program led to only limited success, it began a mind-set of organizing structures that coordinated singular efforts for greater impact. The real strokes of genius were the Rural Community Development Councils (RCDCs), created in the mid-forties, and the Community Development Foundation in 1948. These last two organizing structures allowed the region to move to a different level of work and working together (Grisham, 1999).

The RCDCs were opportunities and vehicles for every rural community in the seven-county area to take hold of its own development. Although TVA, a local college, and other firms provided technical assistance, the expectation was that the community would decide *itself* how it would develop, would assess the improvements that were needed, and then determine its strengths. "The RCDC's were to think about all aspects of community development from education to farm management to housing" (McLean, 1946, quoted in Grisham, p. 95). By the 1950s, there were fifty-six councils, involving six thousand citizens, representing black and white communities. The organizations developed projects that the newspaper would celebrate, and more and more people in the region began seeing their individual success tied to the collective success of their neighbors and their region.

The second big organization (or reorganization) was the elimination of the traditional chamber of commerce and the creation of the Community Development Foundation (CDF). McLean knew that business leadership was critical to Tupelo's success, but not just in the traditional way. McLean put forward the idea that economic development had to be linked to community development. In other words, the region needed an entity that focused on all aspects of the community and not just business development. Reed said that McLean knew that progress depended on a strong community. The idea made sense to people. The Community Development Foundation was formed in 1948 with 151 charter members, with the Rural Community Development Councils as its crown jewel. Communities and organizations began to look at Tupelo as a model for rural development. Former secretary of agriculture, Orville Freeman said, "the best program of rural development I have been exposed to anywhere around the country" (Grisham, 1999, p. 100).

The CDF has met with tremendous success over the last fifty years. It has coordinated, spearheaded, and nurtured development in all areas. It has twelve hundred members and a standing in the region that allows it to represent the community on many fronts. It promotes teamwork and involvement. Businesspeople in Tupelo know that they are expected to give back, join in, and work hard on behalf of the community. According to Michael Clayborne, president of the CREATE Foundation, the community embraced new people through the CDF. There was a high level of expectation also. The organization, the newspaper, and others have recognized the importance of investing at all levels in the community, especially education. The Tupelo public schools represent a key factor in its success and the region's development. The community passed a $30 million school bond issue, the largest in Mississippi's history in 1990 with almost 90 percent approval. It was clear that Tupelo wanted an excellent school system for everybody. There is no tradition of private education in Tupelo.

Race relations in Tupelo have been strained over the years, but progress has been made. Blacks and whites were separated in traditional ways. However, Tupelo was on a mission of broad-based development that needed trained labor—lots of trained labor—to be attractive to firms. The schools were key. Tupelo was the second community in Mississippi to enact school desegregation in 1965, just one day after Greenville. School leaders in Tupelo had wanted to be the first. At a time when segregated academies were springing up in neighboring states and throughout the United States, Tupelo kept its eye on a different strategy—preparing all of its young people to succeed. Schools became a focal point for everybody. Tupelo and Lee

County invested almost three-quarters of a million dollars in a vocational technical center, the University of Mississippi established a branch campus in the region, and McLean created a new community foundation, CREATE, Inc., that would collect funds to support education and other initiatives and also spur local efforts. He ultimately willed the newspaper and its holdings to the foundation. However, the most long-lasting investment by the community would have to be in the K–12 system. McLean himself gave $1 million to place reading aides in every first-grade classroom for a ten-year period. The investment paid off: scores on standardized tests moved nationally from the bottom quarter to the top half (Pittman, 1993).

Partnerships were built between local, regional, and federal organizations to promote all aspects of education, from literacy to job training to faculty development. L. D. Hancock, the founder of Hancock Fabrics, gave $3.5 million to establish an institute for teachers. At the time, it was the largest gift to a public school system in United States history (Pittman, 1993).

There is only one high school in Tupelo for two thousand students in grades 9–12. The school has 134 faculty members on a seventy-five-acre campus. Twice the U.S. Department of Education has named Tupelo High School as a National Blue Ribbon School. The Ford Foundation and Harvard University's Kennedy School of Government recognized Tupelo and the school with one of its prestigious Innovation in Government Awards for the public-private partnership (Grisham, 1999, p. 124). The school system is not only a link to the economic future but also a clear statement that the community is linked—one to another.

Tupelo has done what others said could not be done. They have overcome obstacles, they have literally weathered storms, and they have bridged the fault lines of race and class in ways that other communities have not. The physical and demographic assets they lacked, they made up for with hard work, organization, and strong local leadership. That strong leadership was exemplified by George McLean and other business leaders. Vision, resources, and a willingness to go against the conventional wisdom set a tone and a path for the city and the region that was positive, inclusive, and honest. McLean "tipped the scales" by creating an environment where everyone was expected to lead and contribute. According to Clayborne, "Whether you have assets or not, if you don't have visionary community leaders, you can't enjoy community success." The process of leadership involvement goes beyond a limited circle. Tupelo not only embraces new people, it also has a high level of expectation for them. There is a sense of responsibility that filters through the community. Lots of people, says Clayborne, actively participate in some aspect of community involvement.

One interesting perspective identified by both Reed and Clayborne was the role of the three community banks. Rather than competing against one another in a destructive way, they bought into and acted on the idea that business does well when a community grows and the pie gets bigger for everyone. The working relationships established across the community have been key factors in its success.

The Tupelo story mystifies and intrigues: How have they done it? What's the secret? According to Reed, it was not only key business leadership but also a realization that success was made up of many parts: a newspaper, a first-rate hospital, the public schools. The list goes on. The real secret, of course, was the people themselves and the strength of their collective leadership capacity. Some might think how lucky Tupelo and Lee County are to have added a thousand new manufacturing jobs every year in the last decade. They got lucky because they talked about "the could" not "the can't."

Research Triangle Park: Common Ground for Progress

Perhaps at no time in our history have we needed the resources and expertise of higher education more. There was a time when college and university officials were the catalysts behind visionary social and economic initiatives, both on campus and off. Leaders like Robert Maynard Hutchins, Booker T. Washington, and Charles Elliot set a moral and intellectual tone for the United States, not just for Chicago, Tuskegee, and Cambridge.

The need for academic leadership was clear in a paper Odum wrote recommending common ground, communication, and common action as the remedy to the social problems facing the South, recounts William Friday, president emeritus of the University of North Carolina. Odum talked about a research institute for the development of southern resources, operated by local higher education institutions (Larrabee, 1991, pp. 63–64). Nowhere have those qualities caught fire as they have in Research Triangle Park, North Carolina. One of the smartest decisions ever made in North Carolina was the creation of the Research Triangle Institute and Park in 1959. It was made by a visionary group, including the governor, key business leaders, and the presidents and faculty of three universities: Duke University, North Carolina State University, and University of North Carolina at Chapel Hill.

North Carolina in the fifties was primarily a rural state, whose staples were tobacco, textiles, and furniture manufacturing. It was not unlike its neighbors to the south and west. Its future changed, however, when Governor Luther Hodges heard about a proposal to create a research and development area "triangle" in the Raleigh-Durham-Chapel Hill area. The idea came from several fronts, one being a native North Carolinian, Romeo Guest, an MIT graduate who thought that North Carolina should have its version of Boston's Route 128 or California's Stanford Research Institute. Guest and others piqued the interest of Governor Hodges, as well as that of the three universities. Hodges understood the significance of the possibility, says Friday. Most companies doing sophisticated research were not interested in North Carolina. Their history as a low-tech, rural state, coupled with a perception that the schools, public services, and amenities were lacking, caused most to look elsewhere. However, the governor and the working committee thought differently. As a consultant report observed, "Rather than competing adversely with each other, they [the universities] should add to and enhance the opportunity for development of a major scientific and industrial community" (Larrabee, 1991).

The park started out as a strictly academic enterprise, the Research Triangle Institute. Young entrepreneurial scientists back from World War II saw great potential in the idea to further the research capability of the universities and the region. The usual turf wars never entered the picture, says Friday, because the park was a new idea, not positioned with any one institution; science and technology were not into the turf wars like other disciplines; and the endeavor was incredibly creative. It garnered the attention and support of key faculty and administrators. They were aided by the appointment of George Simpson as executive director of the Research Triangle Committee. Called "one of the heroes" of the effort, Simpson guided the development of the research triangle concept (Larrabee, 1991, p. 8).

Research Triangle Institute was officially created in late 1958, but it took years of commitment from the state, the universities, and the business community for the decision to bear real fruit. There were lean years in the sixties, when some companies backed out, and last-minute loans were required when funds got low. But the leadership, different by now from the original in some cases, stayed the course. The universities still compete mightily for students, for grants, and in athletics, but they all know that their collective futures have been well served by their willingness and ability to work together to develop a regional technology, research, and business park. Now almost a half century later, what are the results? The Research Triangle Institute was the first occupant in Research Triangle Park. It is the fourth-largest nonprofit contract research organization in the United States. As for the park, it has 140 companies and employs almost forty thousand people, with combined annual salaries of $1.2 billion. The research triangle is composed of Raleigh, Durham, and Chapel Hill, but its impact is felt throughout the state and the region. A decision made by a group in 1958 changed North Carolina's fortunes and future (Research Triangle Park Web site).

"The park has gone far beyond its original vision," says Friday. "Although Governor Hodges knew what it could mean, no one thought that it could be what it is today. The early founders, design-ers, and scientists did understand that they had an opportunity to demonstrate a vision of business, government, and higher education that didn't exist anywhere else in the state or region," recalls Friday.

The lessons from the creation of the Research Triangle Park cer-tainly speak volumes about tenacity and vision, but they also speak about the kinds of leaders who could create something as big and bold as a research park in a state dominated by low-wage manufac-turing. It was that *outward* focus by the university presidents (and certainly others) that illustrated what is missing too often today in academia. The *inward* focus on fundraising, public relations, and athletics has left many institutions of higher education at the start-ing gate when it comes to tackling the big issues of our society or (sadly) preparing their students to do so. A second important les-son concerns the time that it takes for investments to yield results. Community, or in this case regional, investing is a long-term strat-egy rather than a quick fix. Friday said that the success of the Research Triangle Park model spilled over into other parts of the economy, including jobs, auxiliary businesses, and the like. The real breakthrough, he believes, will come when we understand that we must invest in people and for the long term. A current example of this strategic thinking, he believes, is the allocation of the tobacco settlement money to create a biotechnology center and the com-mitment to the training of workers for the industry. These kinds of strategic investments are what Friday thinks was a major factor in the success of the Research Triangle. He said that they were always able to "keep strategic thinking well ahead of a crisis."

The three previous examples have illustrated the importance of traditional leaders with vision and persistence. Embedded within these examples are the dedication and work of citizens who have helped craft their own future. The success story of these cities also has the handprints of many civic leaders. In the following example, the work of a group of volunteers in Colquitt, Georgia, to create new opportunities for work, play, and creativity makes a powerful case for leadership from everyone.

Colquitt: We've Got a Story to Tell

What does the ninth poorest congressional district in the United States have to tell others: lots of things. And they do it twice a year to packed audiences. Colquitt, Georgia, is in the southwest corner of Georgia, fifty miles from Tallahassee, Florida, and Dothan, Alabama. In 1990, a local businesswoman, Joy Jinks, heard about the idea of a community play while attending a creativity conference in New York City. The presenter, Richard Geer, was looking for a place to try out his idea. Jinks was intrigued and talked with him further about Colquitt. She and other community leaders had originally wanted to do a historical play about the area, but the story idea was very appealing. The volunteers at the local arts council, where Jinks was a volunteer, thought so too. The idea was powerfully simple: a community records its oral history and produces the stories in a play, citizens in the community are the actors, and the people in the community connect personally in new ways.

A small group of about ten volunteers batted around the idea and thought it just might work. Geer came down from Chicago to begin the planning process. Not everyone in the broader community was sold, however, remembers Karen Kimbrel, executive director of the arts council and one of the movers and shakers to make it happen. "We had to do some consensus building. Some people were afraid it would stir up racial discord or political problems or wake up old ghosts." Others thought the "outsiders" might steal their stories for their own benefit. However, the working group pushed on and tried to allay the fears by assuring the community that it was the "trustee of its stories."

A small grant from the Georgia Humanities Council provided funds for a local team to begin to gather the oral histories. More than a thousand stories have been collected since 1992. The play, named *Swamp Gravy*, after a dish made from fried-fish remnants and vegetables to stretch a meal, was beginning to take shape. The scripts were written by a professional scriptwriter based on the oral histories, volunteers made the sets and costumes, a hundred volunteer performers played the parts, and the local elementary school lent its auditorium. People who had never spoken publicly were belting out lines and songs. The first play, based on the work ethic in the community, was presented in October 1992 to a packed house. Kimbrel says that the message to the community is that "everybody has a gift to give—you have a gift to give."

From the beginning, the volunteer organizers knew that this could bring the community together in new ways; the experience could cross racial and class boundaries that had never been crossed. *Swamp Gravy* has done that and more. The plays have strengthened the community more than anyone could have ever known. Volunteers perform, build sets, make costumes, and greet guests in a restored cotton warehouse, contributing thousands of hours of volunteer time to each play. That first play in the elementary school has grown to two plays a year in October and April, played to sellout crowds in a county that has a total population of 6,500. Thanks to the generosity of a former Colquitt resident, the old cotton warehouse that stood vacant since the boll weevil brought down King Cotton has been transformed into a presentation theater, Cotton Hall.

The Colquitt/Miller Arts Council, the driving force behind *Swamp Gravy*, has branched out into new areas. The idea of "just a community play" has taken on proportions that Jinks and others did not imagine. Says Kimbrel, "We were naïve. We didn't know we couldn't do it" (produce two plays a year and take a giant leap in other areas). That leap meant moving from a budget of $2,000 in 1989 to $1.6 million today. The council has become a driving economic force in the county, employing thirty-five to forty people full-time at any given period. It owns a hotel and restaurant, Tarrer Inn; a skill center, New Life Learning Center, which provides job and life skills as well as traditional craft skills such as quilting and pottery; and another multiuse facility for rehearsals, children's programs, and display areas.

Swamp Gravy, as a community play, has a real track record. Each play is original, written and performed for each of the last ten years, playing to audiences exceeding a hundred thousand. It has become an economic force that allows the arts council to be a major employer in the county. It has revitalized a small downtown with shops, restaurants, and small businesses. It has created a different legacy and a different future for the community. *Swamp Gravy* has built a way for people in the community to use arts and culture to build relationships with each other. According to Kimbrel, "People connect to each other, to place, and to who they are as a person. Once you connect to yourself, place becomes a strong foundation for new development."

Colquitt will never be the same because of a group of volunteers who had enthusiasm for an idea and worked tirelessly to make it happen, because of people in the community who shared their lives and histories, and because of thousands of volunteers who gave up their fears, self-doubts, and time to create something bigger than they ever dreamed. It is a strong case not only for the power of civic leadership but also for the power of inclusiveness. The performers are primarily white, but the number of African Americans in the casts has ranged from 10 to 25 percent. Kimbrel and her colleagues are continually trying to reach out and build trust with the African American community and the larger community through outreach to schoolchildren and seniors and through the conscious solicitation of ideas, stories, and performers.

Even though the play has had dramatic economic effects on the county, there are still large problems looming, like an alarmingly high teen pregnancy rate, poverty, and unemployment. With external funding, the arts council, the schools, and others are tackling those problems too. The script they see for Colquitt does not begin and end with *Swamp Gravy*. It includes a community where people feel connected, have access to opportunity, and want to achieve all they can achieve. As the folks there will tell you, this is just the beginning.

The Colquitt example makes a powerful case for finding leaders in unusual places. The volunteers at the arts council have taken the lead in a way they did not imagine. What began as simply a "good idea" for a community play has grown into an economic and community development strategy that is providing jobs, tourist dollars, and job and life skills. These civic leaders took a risk, and the result is an exciting opportunity for the whole community. As important as the initial "risk" of producing a play was the group's clear understanding of the need to include and empower others around their vision. The lasting impact of *Swamp Gravy* will be its effect on people in the community whose voices were heard for the first time. One performer told me it was her first time on the stage. The case study is not just about ten volunteers who fostered the idea of *Swamp Gravy*. It is about the hundreds of people who have contributed to the success of the project by combining imagination with hard work and action.

Lessons Learned: Looking Broader and Deeper

Part of the challenge of reaching more broadly for new leaders is simply finding them and recruiting them. Often they do not appear on the traditional lists or frequent the same civic club. It is essential that communities call forth the leadership possibilities that exist in people from all circumstances and experiences, reminding them and ourselves that we all are what John Gardner calls "the responsibles," average citizens that work together across boundaries to make their communities better (Gardner, 1997).

No longer is it desirable or even practical to build *leadership pyramids*—those closed, hierarchical structures based on traditional organizational charts. Rather, the task facing communities today is to build *leadership plazas*—open, inviting opportunities to put the whole community to work *for* the community.

Leadership in its truest form is about connecting with others and ultimately catalyzing actions toward common interests. The pyramid model works off the assumption that leaders are few and followers are many. There are certainly times when decisions must be made by a few rather than the many, but the plaza model calls for a process of inclusion, decision making, and action that makes everyone "responsible."

The question then is this: How do we build leadership plazas rather than leadership pyramids? First, we must find ways to recruit and prepare more citizens for active participation. Too few Americans ever have the opportunity for civic-leadership training. Second, we must look in both boardrooms and backyards for leadership bench strength. Third, we must teach and learn new skills, such as consensus building, asset-based development, collaboration, and communication. Finally, we must act on some of the concepts where we often give lip service: concepts such as inclusion and diversity. We need everybody.

Leadership can make all the difference. As these four examples show, the presence of vision and persistence at critical times can create untold possibilities. The message is pretty clear. We need to have higher expectations of traditional leaders, give more opportunities for citizen leaders to participate, and make it business as usual for people to work together. But it is not a one-way street. It is time for communities to decide together the route to success and the way they plan to get there.

Getting Started in Your Community

How is the leadership capacity of your community developed? When are people willing to step up to the plate on important issues? Examples throughout this chapter and throughout the preceding chapters offer some ideas. First, establish places and spaces where leaders at all levels can interact. In Tupelo, it was the Community Development Foundation. In Colquitt, it was the arts council. Think of the places in the community that would be considered neutral convenors.

Second, look at how your community is preparing people for leadership. If you agree that people from across the community have contributions to make, you need to know if training programs are available to them. Everyone needs skills and relationships in order to work effectively for common purposes. A program has been created at the Pew Partnership called LeadershipPlenty, which is aimed at citizens (that would be all of us) who need skills in asset-based community development, strategic partnerships, and conflict management, to name just a few. Every person in America who wants these skills should be able to get them locally.

Third, examine the community's expectations for leadership. Do you punish elected officials for taking the long view and reward them for being myopic? Are citizens expected to be part of the "discussing and deciding" in a community? How is the community structured for leadership? Do you have bench strength?

Fourth, identify the rallying points for broad-based leadership. Many issues touch all people in a community. Leaders need real work to do. There should be plenty for everyone.

Leaders make a difference, as the illustrations in this chapter clearly show. Communities need to think as much about their leadership development as they do about their economic and community development. The results of such a priority will show surprising results.

8

Inventing a Brighter Future

I define innovation as removing barriers to doing what comes naturally, the common sense solutions to our problems.

Paul Light

Ideas and inventions encompass things that are mechanical, social, and civic. Real inventions require a real leap of knowledge, writes Dyson (2001) in his history of inventions. *Civic inventions* must ultimately improve a particular problem or the way we work. Doing something better or more efficiently can often promise the same results, but only quicker! The previous chapters focused on the experience and knowledge gained from the smart decisions of more than twenty communities. The challenge is how to apply this strategic way of thinking in all communities—how to invent a way of making smart decisions that is "based on a leap of imagination" (Dyson, p. 2). Ultimately, inventions are about the future. As Charles Kettering described the difference between most people and inventors, "Most people are interested in where they come from. Inventors are interested in where they are going" (1982, p. 72).

Framing the Issues

All inventions start with a knowledge of what's already out there. They are built on the hard work and tested experience of others. The key to inventing is to assimilate the pieces and parts of the success and apply them to other situations. The case illustrations in preceding chapters provide an excellent view on "what's already out there" (Dyson, 2001, p. 2).

The purpose of this chapter is to synthesize the lessons learned from the seven leverage points that can invent new structures and processes for community decision making. Invention is a critical final piece to the leverage process. Ultimately, every community has to invent what will work for its circumstances. There are no cookie-cutter approaches to systemic change. The recipe for community success rests on the ability to invent the structure, process, and leadership to make long-term change. The preceding chapters show the steps to invent new ways to work together for positive results.

Investing Right the First Time

The community investment strategy suggested in Chapter Two turns on the premise that smart investments pay big dividends in the long term. We looked at dropout prevention as one issue that needs attention and has enormous potential for individual and community return on investment. Keeping a young person in school is a good lifetime investment. Not investing can have disastrous effects down the road.

At the same time, we learned from other chapters that experience has shown that we must be concerned with multiple investment "opportunities." We cannot neglect the physical infrastructure of school buildings, highways, sewers, and bridges—necessary investments, although not glamorous ones. This is where deliberation and leadership come into play. We have to have mechanisms to decide the priorities and the people needed—elected, volunteer, nonprofit, and corporate—to see that these priorities are met. The investment challenge does not begin and end with one set of decisions, as important as that might be. As we saw in several communities, the initial investment decision led to a range of other issues that had to be addressed.

One of the smartest community decisions of the last century had exactly that dilemma. In Minneapolis, the Board of Trade established an independent park commission in the late nineteenth century to preserve and protect parkland and green space. The board believed that securing land then for what they called "the finest and most beautiful system of public parks and Boulevards of any city in America" would add many millions to the future value of real estate in the city (Speltz, cited in Garvin, 1996, p. 64). Despite objections by the city council that the commission lacked accountability and oversight, the voters approved the creation of the commission.

Minneapolis was smart because it established the parks commission, which led to the development of an exquisite park system, but they were *really* smart because they understood that the building of the park was just the start of the expenses. (Think of the original price of a home and then its upkeep over its lifetime!) Minneapolis took into account the broader implications and requirements of its investment and provided the system an income stream, an elected administrative structure, and the legal power to ensure that the parks are maintained (Garvin, 1996, p. 69).

The original investment has paid off. There are six thousand acres in the system: one acre of parkland for every sixty-six citizens, or every home within six blocks of a park. The property and land values of park-adjacent neighborhoods and downtown property have shown enormous increases. Every nickel spent on the parks and green space yields a twenty-fold return (Koerner, 1998). But just as important, the commission has mechanisms to support, preserve, and enhance the original investment.

Investments, even smart ones, need ancillary decisions. The ramifications of one decision often result in the need for shifting other strategies. In the case of dropout prevention, discussed in Chapter Two, it is clear that a one-size-fits-all dropout program will not do the job. The advice given by the school systems in Cedar Rapids and Dallas was a multifaceted approach: an alternative school, access to computer-based learning, additional teachers and counselors, targeted outreach to students and parents, and faculty development. Smart investment decisions require an understanding of the choices necessary, reached by evaluating the expected costs and benefits of the whole investment. The invention we need for community investments considers balance, immediacy, long-term return, necessary auxiliary investments, and risk management.

Working Together

If 90 percent of Americans believe that working together to solve community problems is the best approach, we better listen and we better learn how. The divisiveness of partisan politics and the bureaucratic maze of public policy implementation have made Americans leery of entering the arena of community problem solving. The lines in the sand and the sheer hassle of participating leave people wary and at home.

The challenges that every community faces, even very successful communities, require that we understand better how to work across boundaries. Several very helpful books give specific instructions on how to build community processes that make working together possible and achievable. David Chrislip's *Collaborative Leadership Fieldbook* (2002) gives step-by-step instructions on ways to build collaborations in a community. His framework for collaboration is very helpful in understanding how to structure the process so that it will work. Russell Linden's book *Working Across Boundaries* (2002) spells out the why and the how of collaboration. Linden's discussion of the challenges of collaboration adds realism to the complexity of the process. Even though the "how-to" part of working together is critically important, the hardest part to accomplish is the "want to." It is easier and quicker *not* to work with other people or other organizations. "I just want to get it done," some folks lament. The problem is whether the "it" is the real problem to be addressed. Some of the most intractable problems are disguised as something else. Further, they cannot be affected by one person or one single organization. The challenge for aspiring collaborative efforts is to create a picture of the possibilities for the stakeholders involved. It is not enough to articulate the vision in goals and objectives. People must "see," in a sense, the possible and probable outcome.

The banding together of citizens in Asheville during the eighties to stop the destruction of downtown buildings created a different vision of the community. But working together is about stopping things and starting things too. Colquitt volunteers worked together to start *Swamp Gravy*. Business leaders in Tupelo worked together to create an economic and community development plan that defied all the odds. Certainly, Chattanooga proved that working together can change the future. As approaches to common work are created, people must remember that the currency of ideas galvanizes groups where a process alone cannot. A successful invention for working together must include an issue that counts, a process that is respected, inclusion that is real, and tangible results.

Building on Community Strengths

When I first heard John McKnight describe asset-based community development at a meeting at the Kettering Foundation over a decade ago, I was struck by the commonsense aspect of the whole notion. If people are treated as if they have nothing to contribute—assets— then they are not likely to feel as if they can contribute. It was a powerful breakthrough in my own thinking, so much so that I still have my notes from the meeting. However, tucked deep in the recesses of my mind was a question: Was this simply a vehicle for encouraging the discouraged, or was it a dramatically different way to think and act about the poor and disadvantaged and the neighborhoods where they live? I am firmly in the latter camp. Asset-based community development may be the most important "invention" in the community building field in decades. There are stories of hope and aspiration in places and neighborhoods that had even written *themselves* off as lost causes. When individuals not only have been encouraged but also recognize themselves as a critical variable in the problem-solving process—and not the problem—change happens.

The wonderful work in western North Carolina to help a dozen small towns (many with only one stop light) recognize their assets and be proud of where they live is a clear example of beginning where you are, knowing what you value, and using your assets. The same is true in Denver, where Lower Downtown was an eyesore of viaducts, parking lots, and vacant buildings, and now it is thriving with development, redevelopment, and a future. It was an asset waiting to be found.

Assets are in every person and in every neighborhood. Is this a process for optimists only? No. Asset-based community development is a commonsense way to unlock talents in people, places, and neighborhoods long forgotten. It saves money, saves people, and saves communities. Communities need to invent ways not only to identify assets but also to use them. This requires that we reimagine our way of working and relating to one another.

Practicing Democracy

The notion that public dialogue can solve problems makes perfect sense to community builders. In fact, they know that most smart decisions are built on some form of conversation. We are only beginning to fully grasp the impact on social capital that this kind of dialogue can have. Years of work by the Kettering Foundation and the Study Circles Resource Center shows time and again that dialogue leads communities to different ways of interacting, different relationships, and often different decisions. If we were to analyze each of the case illustrations across all the chapters, we would surely find dialogue in one form or another. None of the smart decisions discussed in the book were made unilaterally. People had to come along, had to be included. When George McLean launched the idea of Rural

Community Development Councils in the region around Tupelo, Mississippi, he knew that he couldn't ramrod the idea through. He met with every opinion leader in the rural areas, and in a pamphlet given to every family in the region he wrote:

> It is unfortunately true that in many parts of America the people have stopped coming together; discussing their mutual problems; assuming their responsibilities; and taking necessary *group action*. Such practices constitute the *essence of democracy* and unless we return to these fundamentals, we shall further endanger our democratic freedom. Maybe we can't revive such practices "in the nation"—but we can make a start in our *local community*. (cited in Grisham, pp. 90–91)

That is the essence of the kinds of inventions that we must have for our communities—a way to have meaningful dialogue as part of everyday life and work.

The conversations in Jacksonville, Hampton, Owensboro, and Wilmington are illustrations of the formalized dialogue process. As they have shown, it is not all just talk; it is connecting, building relationships, and then acting. The invention for embedding community dialogue must include a "starter" issue, but ultimately the dialogue must result in tangible outcomes for its full value to be realized. Communities that can talk together make better decisions.

Preserving the Past

Compared with many societies in the world, America is in its infancy. Many of our oldest buildings are only a few hundred years old, as compared with thousands of years old elsewhere. Nonetheless, we have a past on which to build and learn from. As we saw in the case examples, physical structures can be enormous anchors in communities for restoration and rebuilding. The saving of the mill buildings in Lowell has created an attractive downtown for sure, but it has also ensured that the city holds onto its artistic, economic, and cultural beginnings.

However, the future can also rest on the events or the history of a place, and not necessarily be tied to something physical. The invention that is needed to preserve the past has more to do with *reclaiming* it than it does with *restoring* it. That is not to say that the preservation of buildings is not important—of course, it is. The larger challenge, however, is to reclaim the history and development of a region, just as Birmingham has staked claim to its racial history through the Civil Rights Institute.

Conversations arise quite often in communities about the justification of preserving a house or a building in lieu of taking on a new project. This is a key decision time for communities. The structure cannot be brought back once it is gone, but often the promise of economic development is hard to say no to. In places where they have said no, however, there is little regret. The folks in Colquitt will likely say that having the old cotton warehouse as the renovated Cotton Hall for their performances is a great addition to their work. The past can help create the future.

The elements for the invention that are needed to create the future are probably right before your eyes. Look around. What places, businesses, homes, even trees, define the community? How can those places—like the river in Chimney Rock, the art deco buildings in Asheville, or the part of the city in Lower Downtown Denver—create new possibilities for the future?

Growing Leaders

Leadership is an elusive term. It can be a noun, as in "We need good leadership," or it can be an adjective, as in "She has leadership potential." More often than not, it means one person or a group of people who know what to do and how to achieve a successful outcome. We tend to remember generals who won the critical battles more than those who lost them or great corporate titans that made money rather than those who squandered it.

Our thinking about leadership has evolved from depending on one person or a few people to solve all our problems to realizing that if you want something done, it will take many people. Research Triangle Institute and Park would never have become a reality without key leadership from many organizations, institutions, and individuals.

The responsibility and the outcomes for our communities have lots of shoulders on which to rest. What am I really saying here? First, leadership cannot depend on just a few, yet we still need people in traditional places of influence with integrity, ideas, and the willingness to stick their necks out for a good decision. Mayor Riley in Charleston has made all the difference. Second, we need people in communities to lead neighborhoods, religious organizations, schools, and the shop floor. We need the high road and the long view from all leaders. Finally, we need ways to prepare people to act and react in new ways. We need an invention to grow more leaders.

My grandmother was a quilter. The quilt she made for me three decades ago was a bow-tie design, made from the dresses, shirts, and dusters that had belonged to me and to a host of relatives. I remember her saying that she was "piecing a quilt top" from variegated and seemingly dissimilar materials. Inventing a strategy for leadership, like quilting, is a complex process that takes an appreciation of resources that often can be overlooked. Quilts can be a metaphor for community leadership patterns. There is a place for the predominant design or color, but it wouldn't be a quilt without all the pieces (Pew Partnership for Civic Change, 2002).

As the examples in Chapter Seven demonstrate, we need leaders from all sectors of the community—not placeholders but effective leaders. We need to spend time finding, recruiting, and working with them. Getting good people with honest, inclusive ideas to take on leadership roles of any sort requires that others support their efforts. Too often, when the tough decisions are made—such as taxes, economic development, or budget priorities—we lose our confidence in them and in ourselves. We revert to our need for short-term answers. The time has come to realize that everybody has to be held accountable and responsible for our collective results.

This leads to a question: How can we get more people at the table—what's the invention? The invention is a broad view of leadership preparation. Our goal must be for everyone who wants leadership training to have it. Some say it can't be done. People in Mississippi, South Dakota, West Virginia, and forty other states think otherwise. Organizations within those states have made commitments to provide leadership training to all the citizens who want it through a program called LeadershipPlenty. The leadership invention we need is one that focuses on the skills for taking action, is available to everyone, and reflects the community.

Lessons Learned: Inventing a Brighter Future

The centennial of the invention of flight occurred in 2003. There were celebrations of the evolution of flight from Dayton, to Kitty Hawk, to Washington, D.C. The remarkable thing about the Wright brothers' contraption was that it actually flew. The pieces actually worked in tandem. Applied separately, the leverage points discussed in this book will make a modicum of improvement. Applied together, they have enormous possibilities to change the future for communities. Like the Wright brothers' plane, the pieces fit together.

In his book *To Conquer the Air*, James Tobin (2003) writes of the dogged determination of Wilbur Wright to solve the mysteries of flight. He believed with his heart and mind that airplane flight was possible. That kind of determination is what fuels this book. I believe that communities can be stronger and more successful for everyone if they make smart decisions. We need not accept the conditions and circumstances handed to us. Together we have the intellect, energy, and will to make our communities work better.

Smart communities are smart because they have made tough decisions, included more people in the process, and built on their assets. They did what had to be done, no matter the obstacles. They had vision and persistence. The communities profiled in this book have shown these qualities over and over.

Am I an optimist about communities? You bet. What drives my belief in the framework for smart decisions is the even bigger possibilities. As Wilbur Wright once said to his sister, "My imagination pictures things more vividly than my eyes" (Tobin, 2003, p. 2). We must imagine our communities as places of hope, responsibility, and equality. This will make our possibilities for the future soar.

References

Abbott, C. "Urban America." In L. Luedtyke (ed.), *Making America*. Chapel Hill: University of North Carolina Press, 1992.

Annie E. Casey Foundation. *Safety and Justice for Communities*. Baltimore, Md.: Annie E. Casey Foundation, 1999.

Annie E. Casey Foundation. *Kids Count 2002 Data Book*. Baltimore, Md.: Annie E. Casey Foundation, 2002.

Annie E. Casey Foundation, Ford Foundation, and Rockefeller Foundation. "Building Stronger Communities." (conference report), 1992.

Arendt, H. *Men in Dark Times*. Orlando: Harcourt Brace, 1968.

Asheville Revitalization Commission. "A Revitalized Downtown." August 1978.

Balfanz, R., and Legster, N. *Statistics Underestimate Dropout Numbers*. Cambridge, Mass.: Harvard Graduate School of Education, 2001.

Barrett, M. "The Balancing Act." *Asheville Citizen-Times*, Jan. 28, 2003, p. A14.

Beck, R. "The Ordeal of Immigration in Wausau." *Atlantic Monthly*, April 1994, *274*(5), 84–97.

Beiman, I. "$10 Million Multi-Story Building Proposed for Terminal Station Site." *Birmingham News*, June 30, 1969, pp. 1, 6.

Bellah, R., and others. *Habits of the Heart: Individualism and Commitment in American Life*. Berkeley: University of California Press, 1985.

Berra, Y. *The Yogi Book*. New York: Workman, 1998.

Berry, J., Portnoy, K. E., and Thomson, K. *The Rebirth of Urban Democracy*. Washington, D.C.: Brookings Institution, 1993.

Best Management Practices. [www.bmpcoe.org/bestpractices/internal/chatt/chatt_3.html].

Birmingham Civil Rights Institute. "Annual Report: Birmingham, AL, 2002" (Tenth Anniversary Commemorative Issue). *Vision*, 2002, 3(4).

Bishop, B., and Lisheron, M. "Patents as Measure of City's Success." *Austin American-Statesman*, May 19, 2002. [www.austin360.com/aas/specialreports/citiesofideas/0519patents.html].

Blackwell, A. "Defining Community Building." National Community Building Network. [www.ncbn.org].

Boundary Crossers: Case Studies of How Ten of America's Metropolitan Regions Work. College Park: University of Maryland, Academy of Leadership Press, 1997.

Broder, D. (quoted on City of Charleston Web site: www.ci.charleston.sc.us/bio/html).

Brodie, M. J. Speech given in Japan, 1997. Used by permission.

Bryson, J. M., and Crosby, B. C. *Leadership for the Common Good: Tackling Public Problems in a Shared-Power World.* San Francisco: Jossey-Bass, 1992.

Burt, M. R. *Why Should We Invest in Adolescents?* Washington, D.C.: Urban Institute, 1998.

Center for Community Self-Help Web site: http://www.self-help.org.

Chaskin, R. J., Brown, P., Venkatesh, S., and Vidal, A. *Building Community Capacity.* New York: Aldine de Grayter, 2001.

Chrislip, D. D. *The Collaborative Leadership Fieldbook.* San Francisco: Jossey-Bass, 2002.

Chrislip, D. D., and Larson, C. E. *Collaborative Leadership: How Citizens and Civic Leaders Make a Difference.* San Francisco: Jossey-Bass, 1994.

Coates, J. F. "Impacts We Will Be Assessing in the Twenty-First Century." *Impact Assessment Bulletin*, 1991, 9(4), pp. 8–25.

Collins, R., Waters, E. B., and Dotson, B. A. *America's Downtowns: Growth, Politics and Preservation.* Washington, D.C.: Preservation Press, 1991.

Committee for Economic Development. *Rebuilding Inner-City Communities.* Washington, D.C.: Committee for Economic Development, 1995.

Council on Foundations. *When Community Foundations and Private and Corporate Funders Collaborate.* Washington, D.C.: Council on Foundations, 1995.

Dave, D. S., and Evans, M. R. *The Determination of the Economic Contribution of the Craft/Handmade Industry in Western North Carolina.* Asheville, N.C.: HandMade in America, 1995.

Delgado, G. *Beyond the Politics of Place: New Directions in Community Organizing in the 1990s.* Oakland, Calif.: Applied Research Center, 1997.

Ditmer, J. "Preservation Becomes Profitable." *Denver Post*, Feb. 11, 2001, p. G2.

Downs, A. "Up and Down with Ecology: The Issue Attention Cycle." *Public Interest*, 1972, *12*, pp. 38–50.

Duluth, Minnesota, Web site: www.ci.duluth.mn.us.

Dusack, M. "Twenty-Five Years of Jacksonville Community Council Inc. Makes a Difference." *Neighborhoods*, July–Aug. 2000, pp. 33–35.

Dyson, J. *A History of Great Inventions*. New York: Carroll & Graf, 2001.

Flora, C. B., and Flora, J. "Developing Entrepreneurial Rural Communities." *Sociological Practice*, 1990, 8, pp. 197–207.

Florida, R. *The Rise of the Creative Class: And How It's Transforming Work, Leisure, Community, and Everyday Life*. New York: Basic Books, 2002.

Freedman, P. *What Makes a Solution?* Charlottesville, Va.: Pew Partnership for Civic Change, 2003.

Fremont, California Web site: http://www.ci.fremont.ca.us.

Froslie, E. H. "Diversity Group Observing Tenth Anniversary." *Forum*, Feb. 24, 2003.

Gardner, J. W. *On Leadership*. New York: Free Press, 1990.

Gardner, J. W. "You Are the Responsibles." *Civic Partners: The Search for Solutions*. Charlottesville, Va.: Pew Partnership for Civic Change, 1997, pp. 3–7.

Garvin, A. *The American City: What Works, What Doesn't*. New York: McGraw-Hill, 1996.

Gates, V. "The Birmingham Civil Rights Institute." *Alabama Heritage*, Fall 2002, pp. 17–25.

Gladwell, M. *The Tipping Point*. New York: Little, Brown, 2000.

Gray, B. *Collaborating: Finding Common Ground on Multiparty Problems*. San Francisco: Jossey-Bass, 1989.

Green, G. P., and Haines, A. *Asset Building and Community Development*. Thousand Oaks, Calif.: Sage, 2002.

Grisham, V. L., Jr. *Tupelo: Evolution of a Community*. Dayton, Ohio: Kettering Foundation Press, 1999.

Grogan, P. S., and Proscio, T. *Comeback Cities*. Boulder, Colo.: Westview Press, 2000.

Halpern, R. *Rebuilding the Inner City*. New York: Columbia University Press, 1995.

Hammer, Siler, George Associates. *Economic Impact of Historic District Regulation*. Washington, D.C.: Forum: National Trust for Historic Preservation, 1990.

HandMade in America. Internal Correspondence. 1995.

Harvard University. *Dropouts in America*. The Civil Rights Project (Series of papers). Cambridge, Mass: Harvard University, 2001.

Harwood Group. *Citizens and Politics: A View from Main Street America*. Dayton, Ohio: Kettering Foundation, 1991.

Harwood Group. *Planned Serendipity*. Charlottesville, Va.: Pew Partnership for Civic Change, 1998.

Henton, D., Melville, J., and Walesh, K. *Grassroots Leaders for a New Economy: How Civic Entrepreneurs Are Building Prosperous Communities.* San Francisco: Jossey-Bass, 1997.

"Heritage Tourism and the Federal Government: Summit I—Report of Proceedings." Washington, D.C.: Advisory Council on Historic Preservation, Nov. 14, 2002. [www.achp.gov/pubs-heritagetourismsummit.html].

Himmelman, A. T. "Communities Working Collaboratively for Change." In M. Herrman (ed.), *Resolving Conflict: Strategies for Local Government.* Washington, D.C.: International City-County Management Association, 1994, pp. 24–47.

Himmelman, A. T. "Collaboration for Change." (revision of existing work), Nov. 2002.

Hunter, E. C., and McGill, K. Y. *Small Voices, Big Songs.* Asheville, N.C.: Hand-Made in America, 1999.

Isaacs, W. *Dialogue and the Art of Thinking Together.* New York: Doubleday, 1999.

Jacobs, J. *The Death and Life of Great American Cities.* New York: Vintage Books, 1961.

Janosz, M., Le Blanc, M., Boulerice, B., and Temblay, R. E. "Disentangling the Weight of School Dropout Predictors: A Test of Two Longitudinal Samples." *Journal of Youth and Adolescence,* 1997, 26(6), pp. 733–763.

Jefferson, Texas, Web site: www.jefferson-texas.com/history.htm.

Jordan, W., and McPartland, J. *Essential Components of High School Dropout Prevention Reforms.* Baltimore: Johns Hopkins University Press, 1994.

Kaufman, P. "Federally Reported Data Underestimate Minority Dropouts." Cambridge, Mass.: Harvard Graduate School of Education (Civil Rights Project), 2001.

Kaufman, P., McMillan, M., and Sweet, D. (eds.). *A Comparison of High School Dropout Rates in 1982 and 1992* (NCES 96-893). Washington, D.C.: U.S. Department of Education, National Center for Education Statistics, 1996.

Kelly, M. "Terminated Station: The Rise and Fall of Birmingham's Terminal Station." *Black and White,* May 28, 1998, pp. 14–17.

Kerner Commission. *Report of National Advisory Commission on Civic Disorders.* Washington, D.C.: Kerner Commission, 1968, cited in R. Halpern, *Rebuilding the Inner City,* 1995.

Kettering, C. F. *Kettering Digest.* Dayton, Ohio: Reflections Press, 1982.

Kettering Foundation. *Communities That Work.* Dayton, Ohio: Kettering Foundation, 1998.

Kettering Foundation. *Making Choices Together: The Power of Public Deliberation.* Dayton, Ohio: Kettering Foundation, June 2002.

Klein, W. R., Benson, V. L., Anderson, J., and Herr, J. B. "Visions of Things to Come." *Planning*, 1993, 59(5), pp. 10–19.

Koerner, B. J. "Cities That Work." *U.S. News and World Report*. June 8, 1998, 124(22), pp. 30, 31.

Kretzmann, J., and McKnight, J. *Building Communities from the Inside Out: A Path Toward Finding and Mobilizing a Community's Assets*. Evanston, Ill.: Center for Urban Affairs and Policy Research, Northwestern University, 1993.

Kuhn, T. *The Structure of Scientific Revolutions*. Chicago: University of Chicago Press, 1996.

Larrabee, C. X. *Many Missions: Research Triangle Institute's First Thirty-One Years— 1959–1990*. Research Triangle Park, N.C.: Research Triangle Institute, 1991.

Larsen, L. H. *The Urban South: A History*. Lexington: University Press of Kentucky, 1990.

Linden, R. *Working Across Boundaries: Making Collaboration Work in Government and Nonprofit Organizations*. San Francisco: Jossey-Bass, 2002.

Lisheron, M., and Bishop, B. "Austin's Fast-Growing Immigrant Community Is Source of Wealth." *Austin American-Statesman*, June 9, 2002. [www.austin360.com/aas/specialreports/citiesofideas/0609immigration.html].

Logan, J. R., and Rabrenovic, G. "Neighborhood Associations: Their Issues, Their Allies, and Their Opponents." *Urban Affairs Quarterly*, 1990, 26(1), pp. 68–94.

"Lowell's Cambodian Community." [http://www.asianbc.com/users/cmaa/communi.html].

Lowell Historical Park Web site: http://www.nps.gov/lowe/loweweb/Lowell_History/rebirth.html.

Lucy, W. *Downtown Revitalization: Charlottesville, Virginia*. City of Charlottesville, 2002.

Luke, J. S. *Catalytic Leadership: Strategies for an Interconnected World*. San Francisco: Jossey-Bass, 1998.

Marye, T. "The New Terminal Station, Birmingham, Ala." *American Architect*, XCVI(1751), July 14, 1909, pp. 13–17.

Mathews, D. *Politics for People: Finding a Responsible Voice*. (2nd ed.) Urbana: University of Illinois Press, 1999.

McNulty, R. H. "Quality of Life and Amenities as Urban Investments." In H. Cisneros (ed.), *Interwoven Destinies: Cities and the Nation*. New York: Norton, 1993.

Michigan Historic Preservation Network. "Investing in Michigan's Future: The Economic Benefits of Historic Preservation." [www.mhpn.org].

Monkkonen, E. *America Becomes Urban: The Development of U.S. Cities and Towns, 1780–1980*. Berkeley: University of California Press, 1988.

Morrison, C. "Housing Prices Soar." *Asheville Citizen-Times*, Jan. 27, 2003, pp. A1, A5.

Morse, S. *Building Collaborative Communities*. Charlottesville, Va.: Pew Partnership for Civic Change, 1996.

National Congress for Community Economic Development. *Coming of Age: Trends and Achievements of Community-Based Development Organizations*. Washington, D.C.: National Congress for Community Economic Development, 1999.

National Trust for Historic Preservation. [www.nationaltrust.org].

Norrell, R. J. *The Alabama Story*. Tuscaloosa, Al.: Yellowhammer Press, 1993.

Oldenburg, R. *The Great Good Places: Cafes, Coffee Shops, Community Centers, Beauty Parlors, General Stores, Bars, Hangouts, and How They Get You Through the Day*. New York: Paragon House, 1989.

Peirce, N. R. "Should People or Places Come First?" *National Journal*, Jan. 16, 1993, p. 150.

Peirce, N. R., and Guskind, R. *Breakthrough*. New Brunswick, N.J.: Center for Urban Policy Research, Rutgers University, 1993.

Pepper, J. "Business Needs to Be at the Table." In *Making Community Solutions Work: What Will It Take?* Charlottesville, Va.: Pew Partnership for Civic Change, 2002.

Pew Partnership for Civic Change. *Just Call It Effective*. Charlottesville, Va.: University of Richmond, 1998.

Pew Partnership for Civic Change. *In It for the Long Haul: Community Partnerships Making a Difference*. Charlottesville, Va.: University of Richmond, 2001b.

Pew Partnership for Civic Change. *What We Know Works*. Charlottesville, Va.: University of Richmond, 2001b.

Pew Partnership for Civic Change. *Crafting a New Design for Civic Leadership*. Charlottesville, Va.: University of Richmond, 2002.

Pew Partnership for Civic Change. *What Will It Take? Making Headway on Our Most Wrenching Problems*. Charlottesville, Va.: University of Richmond, 2003.

Pitkin, H. "Justice: On Relating Public and Private." *Political Theory*, 1981, 9(3), pp. 327–352.

Pittman, D. *Tupelo: Vision at the Crossroads*. Tupelo, Miss.: CREATE, Inc., 1993.

Porter, M. "The Competitive Advantage of the Inner City." *Harvard Business Review*, 73(3), May–June 1995, pp. 55–71.

Potter, J. G. *Great American Railroad Stations*. New York: Wiley, 1996.

Price, W. "Architectural Review Board Handbook." Preservation Alliance of Virginia. [www.vapresearvation.org].

Putnam, R. *Making Democracy Work: Civic Traditions in Modern Italy.* Princeton: Princeton University Press, 1993.

Putnam, R. *Bowling Alone: The Collapse and Revival of American Community.* New York: Simon & Schuster, 2000.

Rabinovitz, F. *City Politics and Planning.* Rockaway Beach, N.Y.: Lieber-Atherton, 1969.

Ready, M. *Asheville—Land of the Sky.* Northridge, Calif.: Western North Carolina Historical Association/Windsor Publications, 1986.

Research Triangle Park Web site: http://www.rtp.org.

Rebchook, J. "Lower, Upper Downtown: A Tale of Two Office Markets." *Rocky Mountain News*, Mar. 18, 2003.

Richardson, C. "Terminal Awaits Last 'All-Aboard.'" *The Birmingham News*, Jan. 13, 1969, pp. 1–2.

Rubin, H. J. *Renewing Hope Within Neighborhoods of Despair: The Community-Based Development Model.* Albany: State University of New York Press, 2000.

Rubin, H. J., and Rubin, I. S. *Community Organizing and Development.* (2nd ed.) Boston: Allyn & Bacon, 1992.

Rural LISC Web site: www.ruralisc.org

Rusk, D. *Cities Without Suburbs.* Baltimore: Johns Hopkins University Press, 1993.

Rypkema, D. D. *The Economic Benefits of Historic Preservation: A Community Leader's Guide.* Washington, D.C.: National Trust for Historic Preservation, 1994.

Sampson, R. J. "What 'Community' Supplies." In R. Ferguson and W. T. Dickens (eds.), *Urban Problems and Community Development.* Washington, D.C.: Brookings Institution Press, 1999.

Save the Children. *America's Forgotten Children: Child Poverty in Rural America.* Westport, Conn.: Save the Children, 2002.

Scherman, T. "The Music of Democracy." *American Heritage*, Oct. 1995, cited in *Utne Reader*, Mar.–Apr. 1996, pp. 29–36.

Senge, P. *The Fifth Discipline.* New York: Doubleday, 1990.

Sirianni, C., and Friedland, L. *Civic Innovation in America.* Berkeley: University of California Press, 1999.

Speltz, S. M. *The Minneapolis Park and Recreation System.* (unpublished reports), 1987, cited in Garvin, *The American City: What Works, What Doesn't*, 1996, p. 64.

Sullivan, W. *Reconstructing Public Philosophy.* Berkeley: University of California Press, 1982.

"Ten Years of Doing Good Work." (editorial) *Forum*, Feb. 26, 2003.

Thorpe, R. Speech presented to Providence Civic Entrepreneurs, 1998.

Tobin, J. *To Conquer the Air: The Wright Brothers and the Great Race for Flight.* New York: Free Press, 2003.

Tsongas, P. *Congressional Record.* (quoted on Lowell Historical Park Web site: http://www.nps.gov/lowe/loweweb/Lowell_History/rebirth.html).

Tupelo Web site: http://www.ci.tupelo.ms.us.

Tyler, N. *Historic Preservation: An Introduction to Its History, Principles, and Practice.* New York: Norton, 2000.

U.S. Bureau of the Census. "Small Area Income and Poverty Estimates Program," 1997.

U.S. Bureau of the Census. "Population, Housing Units, Area, and Diversity: 2000." (Census 2000 Summary File 1), [http:www.census.gov].

U.S. Bureau of the Census. "Percentage of Population Without a High School Diploma," 2002 [http:www.census.gov].

U.S. Department of Education. "New Report Shows Dropout Rates Have Remained Stable over Last Decade," 2001. [http://www.ed.gov/PressReleases/11-2001/11152001.html].

Virginia Department of Historic Resources Web site: http://www.dhr.state.va.us/.

Wacquant, L., and Wilson, W. J. "The Cost of Racial and Class Exclusion in the Inner City." *Annals of the American Academy of Political and Social Science,* 1989, *501*, pp. 8–25.

Wausau, Wisconsin, Web site: www.ci.wausau.wi.us.

White, M., and White, L. *The Intellectual Versus the City.* Cambridge, Mass.: Harvard University Press and MIT Press, 1962.

Williams, M., and Boyle, J. "From Ghost Town to Boom Town." *Asheville Citizen-Times,* Jan. 26, 2003, pp. A1, A5.

Yankelovich, D. *The Magic of Dialogue: Transforming Conflict into Cooperation.* New York: Simon & Schuster, 1999.

Index